SECRET
CARMARTHEN

Dean Hollands

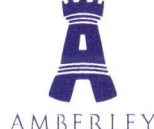

AMBERLEY

Nid oes ffordd well i anrhydeddu pobl Caerfyrddin ddoe a heddiw na chysegru'r llyfr hwn i'w hangerdd, penderfyniad, a dyfalbarhad. Drwy gydol hanes mae eu gweithredoedd a'u geiriau wedi trawsnewid y dref hynafol hon i'r lle hudolus, ysbrydoledig a herfeiddiol ydyw heddiw. Diolch yn fawr iawn.

There is no better way to honour the people of Carmarthen past and present than to dedicate this book to their passion, determination, and perseverance. Throughout history their deeds, words and actions have transformed this oldest of towns into the magical, inspiring, and provocative place it is today. Thank you very much.

First published 2025

Amberley Publishing
The Hill, Stroud
Gloucestershire, GL5 4EP

www.amberley-books.com

Copyright © Dean Hollands, 2025

The right of Dean Hollands to be identified as the
Author of this work has been asserted in accordance
with the Copyrights, Designs and Patents Act 1988.

ISBN 978 1 4456 8461 1 (print)
ISBN 978 1 4456 8462 8 (ebook)

British Library Cataloguing in Publication Data.
A catalogue record for this book is available from the
British Library.

Origination by Amberley Publishing.
Printed in Great Britain.

Appointed GPSR EU Representative: Easy Access
System Europe Oü, 16879218
Address: Mustamäe tee 50, 10621, Tallinn, Estonia
Contact Details: gpsr.requests@easproject.com, +358
40 500 3575

Contents

Foreword

I wish to congratulate Dean with his research and commitment that has led to the publication of this book about the historic town of Carmarthen.

We are often bombarded with local, national, and international events that are impacting on our lives. However, we are often ignorant of the traditions that have shaped our communities. Although I have lived in Carmarthen for the past forty-seven years, I will not be accepted as one of its true residents because I was not born within the walls. However, I am fortunate to be married to Tina, a Carmarthen girl, and this allows me a degree of credibility.

It is an honour to represent Carmarthen as Mayor for the second time, which allows me the opportunity to applaud, encourage and support those selfless persons who are continuing the noble tradition of helping those in greater need on a daily basis.

As the oldest town in Wales, Carmarthen has an abundance of history that deserves to be recognised. My Welsh and Italian heritage gives me great pride and allows me to say that the Romans are still in Carmarthen.

I hope you enjoy the revelations presented by Dean.

Councillor Emlyn Schiavone
Mayor of Carmarthen, May 2024

Introduction

'Above all, watch with glittering eyes the whole world around you because the greatest secrets are always hidden in the most unlikely places.'

Roald Dahl

Carmarthen, Caerfyrddin – so good, they named it twice; well not quite, but for several centuries it existed as two separate towns. Long before that, it was the civic capital of the ancient Celtic Demetae tribe.

When the Roman army arrived in Carmarthen, they fortified the town and built a seaport that enabled large-scale transportation of commercial goods. The town became a prosperous trading settlement and during the centuries that followed Carmarthen became a thriving maritime port, serving as a gateway for trade and commerce into west Wales and beyond. Success brought encounters with pirates, smugglers, press gangs and ship wreckers and the infamous 'Carmarthen Mob'.

For periods of time levels of lawlessness were so bad the town was often compared to a frontier town in the Wild West. Political corruption and wrongdoing earned Carmarthen the title of 'the most politically corrupt borough in the Kingdom'.

Crime and punishment feature strongly in the town's history; its various institutions and gaols bear witness to the grim inhuman conditions and the terror and torment offenders experienced at the hands of nefarious magistrates and inept gaolers. Carmarthen became known as the 'Hanging Town' because hundreds of people were executed. Among the mass of executions, the public witnessed highwaymen hang, smugglers swing, and a bishop burn.

The town, home to both a priory and a friary, has a religious history strewn with accounts of oppression, persecution, and suppression, secret meetings and acts of expulsion, incarceration, and martyrdom. It also became a bastion of Nonconformity when powerful and enigmatic preachers lived in Carmarthen. Among the best known is Reverend Morgan John Rhys, the 'Welsh Baptist Hero of Civil and Religious Liberty of the Eighteenth Century'.

Towards the end of the eighteenth century, turbulent times saw the town fail to secure a parliamentary election, leading to weeks of rioting, and regular soldiers were deployed to restore order. During the Rebecca Riots of 1839–43 police officers were drafted in from London and cavalry with sabres drawn to regain control. By contrast the town became known as 'the Athens of Wales' due to being the Welsh centre of printing and a principal seat of early education. Pioneers of enterprise and endeavour pushed boundaries and set standards that are reflected today in the ceremonies and civic pride displayed by its people, politicians and in the town council's motto 'Rhyddid, Hedd a Llwyddiant' – 'Freedom, Peace and Prosperity'.

Few towns in Wales have a more patriotic story than Carmarthen. The compilation of the 'Black Book' 800 years ago, the re-establishment of the National Eisteddfodau, the pursuits of druids, bards, social activists, and political agitators in preserving and promoting Welsh culture and language are second to none. In 1966 Carmarthen elected the first Welsh Nationalist MP, which started the road to devolution in Wales and Scotland.

This book has been written for the residents of Carmarthen, both long-standing and recently arrived, and those intending to visit this most ancient and interesting of places.

The content has been carefully selected and serves several functions. In this age of social media, information previously not readily available is now generously shared amongst like-minded people. For those with a keen and enthusiastic interest in the people, places and events that have shaped the borough, the title 'Secret Carmarthen' may seem rather misleading as few things about the town and its past are truly secret.

That said, within these pages readers will find many interesting facts about the borough's history and its heritage still waiting to be discovered and others rediscovered. Some are forgotten, others are hidden and hard to find, some exist in plain sight, their significance overlooked.

These secrets are waiting for you here. I hope this book will inspire you to learn more about the borough's history and take time, not only to visit the locations and sites mentioned, but to explore further and find new places and interesting facts of your own to share with others.

1. Past Ports, and Maritime Trading

Carmarthen's main trade and commerce route to the outside world today is via its motorways and arterial roads and before that the railway performed this role. In the early nineteenth century an improved road system was brought about by introducing turnpikes and tollgates to the rough, rock-strewn byways, remnants of ancient tracks dating back to Roman times that begrudgingly afforded passage on foot or horseback.

Before roads, rail tracks and motorways, Carmarthen was isolated on its landward sides, so its only commercial contact with the world beyond was via the River Tywi. Long before the Roman warships of the Classis Britannica (British Fleet) arrived, indigenous people used coracles and small ships for trading with other tribes in and around Carmarthen Bay and along the west coast. Archaeologists' discovery of artifacts has revealed the existence of trade routes between Ireland and Carmarthen used for the importation of copper, bronze, and gold via the Tywi and Taf estuaries. These routes avoided South Pembrokeshire's treacherous rocky coastline.

When the civic capital of the Demetae tribe came under Roman rule between 47 and 48 CE, the entire region became Romanised. Waterways were important to the Romans, who used them to control their empire by transporting officials, goods, troops, and correspondence. Because of its strategic position on the peninsula overlooking the upper tidal reaches of the River Tywi and with easy access to Carmarthen Bay and the Bristol Channel, the Romans built the first seaport in Carmarthen for the large-scale transportation of commercial goods. Records show that the Roman navy navigated the length of the Tywi and would have made use of the port during their patrols.

To protect the port and town they also erected a military fort on the area covered today by King Street and Spilman Street. By the second century a significant and prosperous trading settlement had developed and the Demetae capital 'Moridunum', which translates as 'sea fort', became a Roman *civitas,* one of only two in Wales.

Throughout the Middle Ages smaller quays and riverbanks along the Taf and Tywi estuaries were also used to move cargoes of various kinds to ports in Bristol, Devon, Somerset, and other south coast ports. In peacetime, ships from France, Spain, and Portugal imported wine to the town and records show that in 1284 King Edward I supplied an allowance of 'twenty tuns of wine' (5,120 gallons) for soldiers stationed at the castle which arrived by ship from Bristol.

A medieval system of trade and taxation required that overseas trade of certain goods should be transacted at designated market towns or ports, called staple ports, and in 1353 Edward III declared Carmarthen to be the sole Staple Port of Wales. These ports had the right for merchant barges or ships to unload their goods, and display them for sale for a prescribed period, usually three days, before going to market.

The importance of the town as a port was recognised by Henry VIII, who, by way of charter in 1546, conferred the title of Admiral of the Port of Carmarthen on the mayor. The mayor's main role was to ensure that the river remained free from obstruction and nuisances. Until 1835 the mayor held a ceremonial 'Court of Admiral's Day' when he and members of the corporation were officially sworn in before the mayor and members of the corporation voyaged down to the bar of the Tywi inspecting the river. This custom, revived in 1971, continues today, with members of the River Tywi Yacht Club conveying the mayor and his guests on their inspection of the river. The symbol of Carmarthen's authority over the River Tywi is a silver oar.

During the Middle Ages, the coastal and overseas trade was conducted through Kidwelly, Laugharne and Carmarthen. Carmarthen was tasked with provisioning the castles in the area and on occasion, goods were landed at Green Castle some 2 miles downriver and transported by barges on the River Tywi or on waggons to the town.

The staple export commodities were wool, fleeces, hides, pelts, leather, lead, and tin. The main imports included red and white wines, salt, salted fish, fresh and dried fruits, sugar, spices, oil, tar, silk, and velvet. This situation remained unchanged until the sixteenth century when Carmarthen became a centre for the exportation of wool and woollen yarn. Between 1566 and 1603 port records provide detailed accounts of the ships arriving and leaving the port and their cargos.

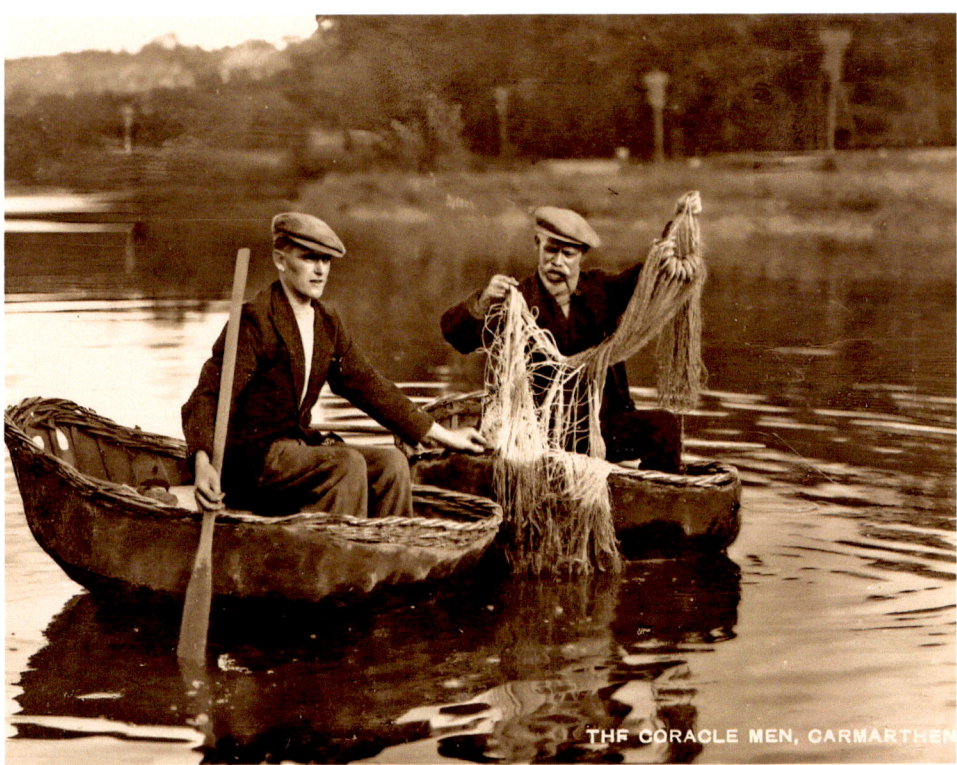

Coracle fishermen.

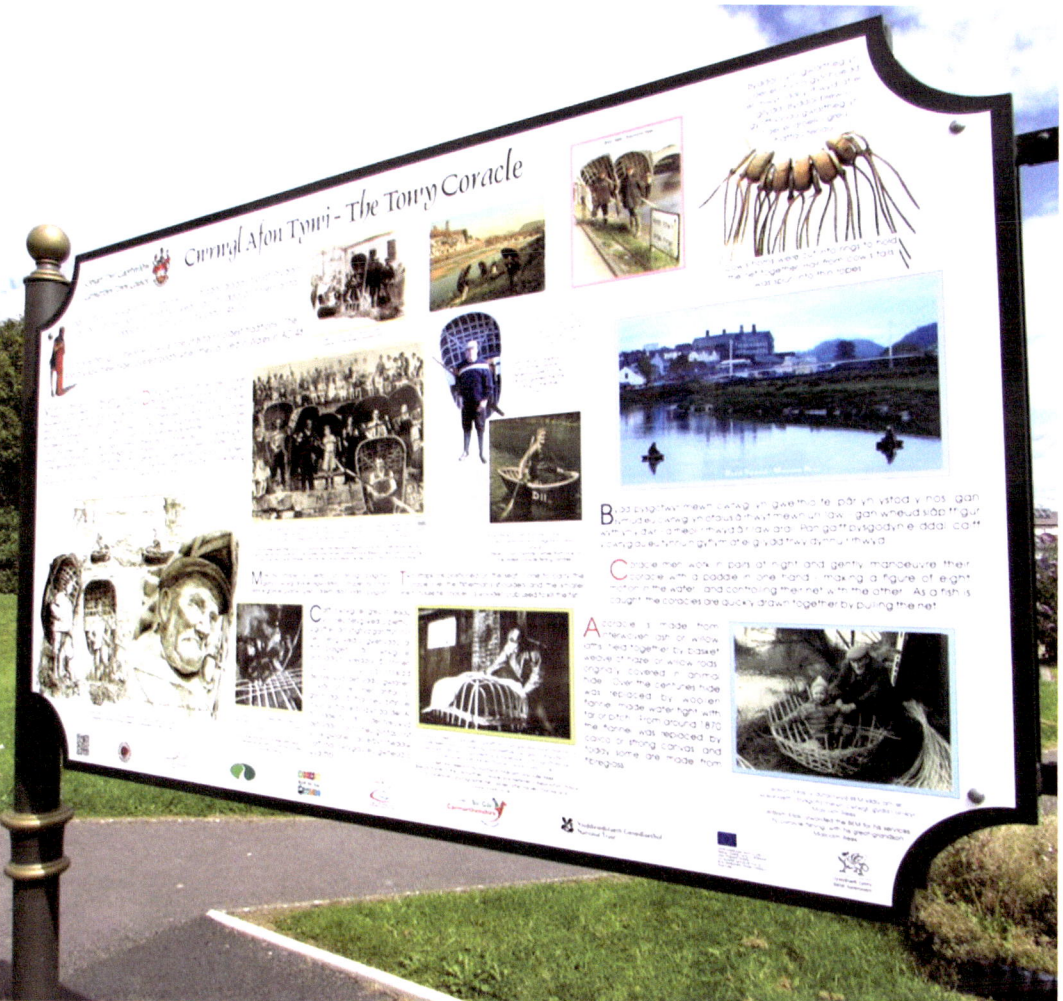

Towy Coracle information board.

DID YOU KNOW?
Pirates were a constant threat to shipping in the Bristol Channel. They'd often wait off the coast to board ships heading towards or leaving Carmarthen. In 1587 a French ship seized by pirates arrived at Carmarthen laden with salt. The pirates auctioned both the ship and its cargo to the highest bidder. In 1592 Carmarthen merchants complained to the Privy Council in London about pirates who robbed them of 'silks, wine and oil to the value of £10,000' (equivalent to more than £1.2 million today). Apart from the pirates, there were Carmarthen smugglers, who received goods from French sailors anchored off the coast for disposal to contacts inland.

Following an anonymous tip-off, the notorious smuggler Dai Davies was ambushed by customs officers at Johnstown near the Royal Oak Tollgate as he drove his cart laden with smuggled spirits. Davies spurred his horse at a gallop with customs in hot pursuit up the hill and past the Picton monument. Having put a respectable distance between himself and his pursuer by some wanton driving through the town and over the bridge, he eventually made good his escape.

Dai continued to outwit and outflank customs officials until his last escapade at Pembroke when the vessel in which he sailed was apprehended by a revenue cutter. He attempted to avoid capture by jumping overboard but drowned in the waters where he had made so much of his fortune.

As the centuries passed changes in Britain's social, economic, and industrial needs were reflected in the goods being exported and imported. The establishment of the landed gentry during the seventeenth century saw ships arriving in Carmarthen laden with luxury commodities such as soap, vinegar, sugar, fruit, pickled herrings, and marmalade, along with furniture, jewellery, games, and toys. Exports now focussed on eggs, slate, bark, bricks, lead ore, and local timber. During the 1720s fifty-seven commercial ships were registered to Carmarthen, and the tonnage of goods in and out of the port was three times the tonnage of the twenty-two vessels registered to Cardiff.

Ship building became a prominent feature of the town's industry before steam and iron-clad vessels were common. Between 1808 and 1809 the quay was lengthened from

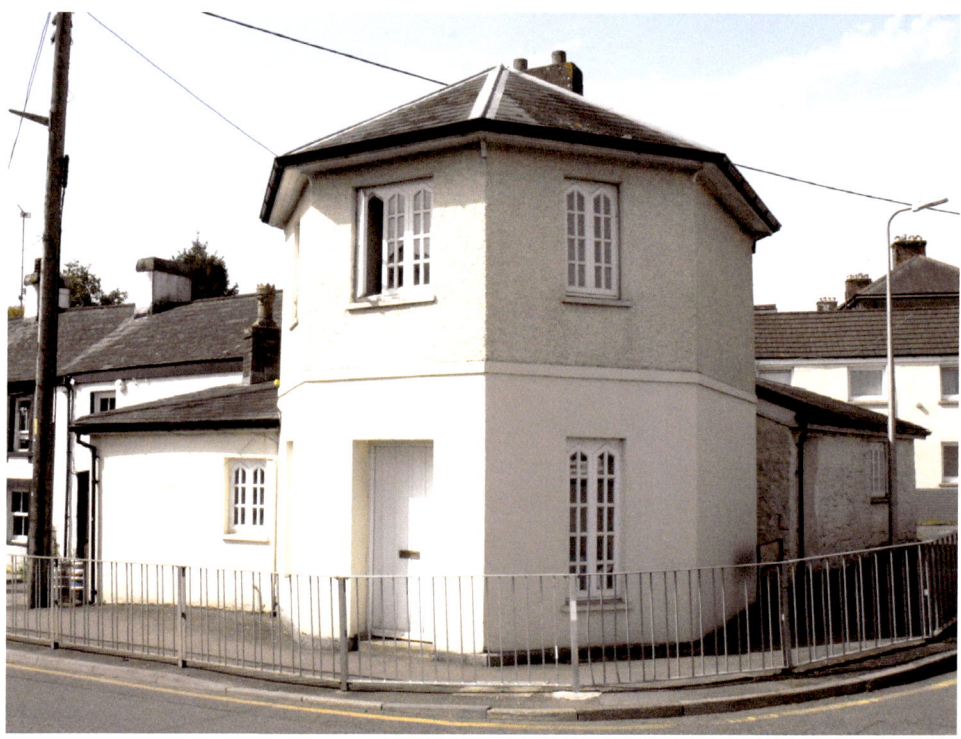

Royal Oak Tollhouse, Johnstown.

the Jolly Jack Tar Ale House to the town bridge and a new dock was built connecting Bedford Yard and the Pothouse Bank to the west of Island Wharf. Here small ships of 200–300 tons of the brig and barque design were built and launched. Sixty such vessels were registered to Carmarthen.

Royal Navy press gangs often roamed the streets of Carmarthen in search of able-bodied men for naval service. One night in 1803, two years before Napoleon's French fleet was defeated by Lord Nelson at Trafalgar, the infamous 'Carmarthen Mob' (a self-appointed group of rebels and vigilantes) mobilised to repel Royal Naval attempts to press Carmarthen residents into service. The *Polly*, a tender from a 'Man of War' anchored in Carmarthen Bay, arrived on the shores having rowed upriver under muffled oars. The press gang were scouring the streets when the alarm was raised, and the town bell rang out a warning.

The Carmarthen Mob began forming their own gangs and scoured the town for the press gang. Amongst them were a number of women who didn't want to lose their husbands! Fearing they'd lynch the sailors, Mayor Paxton began swearing in large numbers of special constables. As daybreak arrived the Carmarthen Mob found the press gang and chased them onto the river, hurling insults and missiles. Out rowed, they gave up their chase, knowing no unwilling recruits had been taken.

While press gangs presented a threat to men on land and pirates and smugglers to cargos and sailors at sea, two other dangers often threatened cargoes and the lives of Carmarthen sailors. First, the elements were deadly, and nineteenth-century records show Carmarthen Bay's sands were treacherous, particularly during violent storms, causing many ships to be wrecked, and cargo and men to be lost.

Other shipwrecks had more sinister origins. The removal of navigational buoys and the lighting of false beacons upon the estuary shores by wreckers claimed many a ship, crew, and cargo. The 'Dynion y Bwyelli Bach' (Men of Little Axes) were infamous wreckers and plunderers, and by design or default they were always first to salvage goods from wrecked or stranded ships.

From miles around they came, working with packhorses and carts. The forlorn wreck was often stripped bare before the authorities realised the disaster. In the absence of any effective law, deterring and apprehending would-be offenders or suspects fell to the military. When the drummer boy sounded the alarm, the men of the Royal Carmarthenshire Militia rapidly gathered at the town centre where they were issued a musket, ten rounds of ball cartridge, and a good flint. Following which, they were dispatched at speed to engage those concerned in the wrecking or plundering of the stricken vessel.

In December 1886 five such persons were caught by the militia and successfully prosecuted for plundering a wreck, the *Teviotdale*, and pillaging the bodies of the sixteen crew members washed upon the shore following a violent storm.

During the 1830s over 400 small British trading vessels and thirteen foreign ships docked at Carmarthen's Quay and the 1840s saw the zenith of the port's trading activities. The principal exports were British timber, bark, marble, slate, bricks, lead-ore, leather, manufactured goods, grain, butter, and eggs but the port was also popular with steam packets and sail ships. The chief imports were foreign timber, pitch, rosin, tallow,

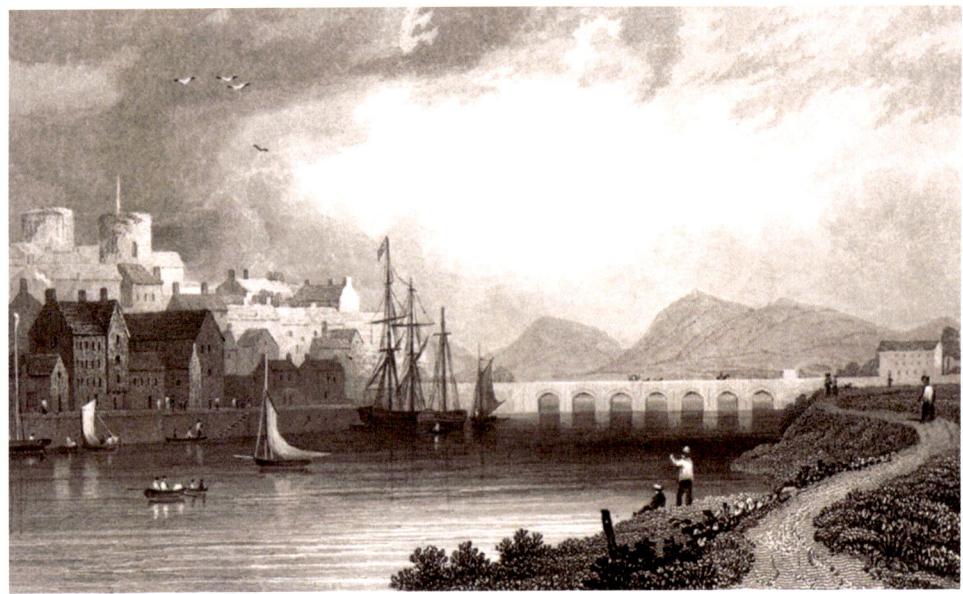

Quay, *c.* 1835. (HG)

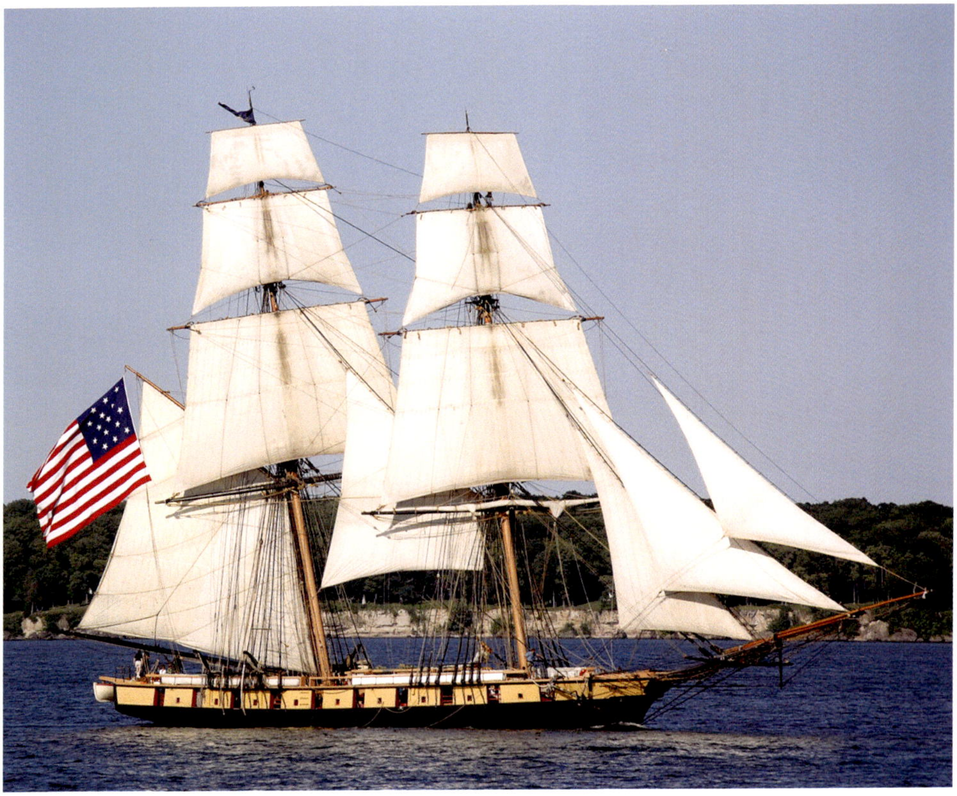

Brig sailing vessel. (LW)

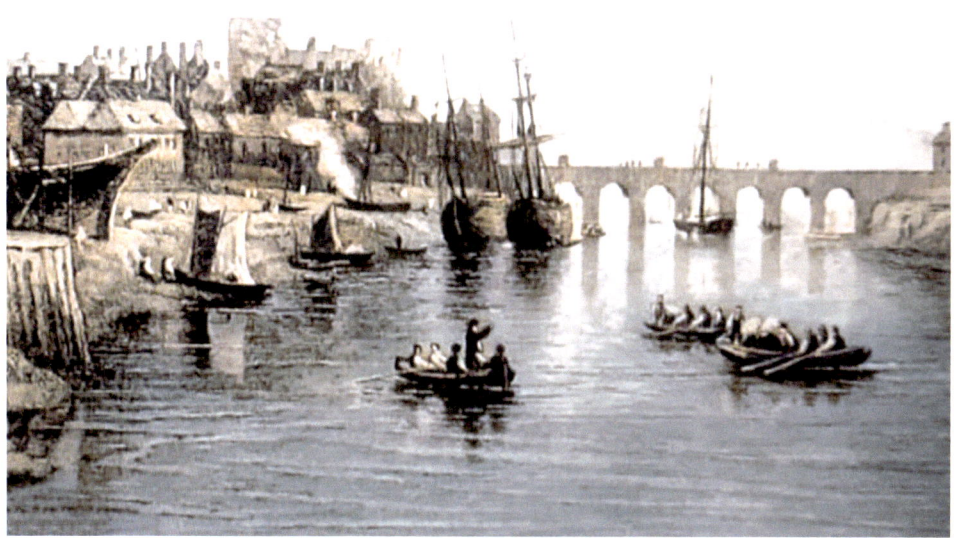

Quay, *c*. 1840. (PD)

coal, culm, malt, and certain manufactured goods sold in the town or supplied to the surrounding area. A forest of masts and rigging was not an uncommon sight as flotillas of up to a dozen American brigs anchored along the river.

Despite such success, the port's reign as king of passenger and freight services, and of import and export for the county – if not the country – was diminishing. As was the power of its princes, the stagecoach and paddle steamer. All would succumb to the advances of the industrial revolution and, of course, the iron road – the railways.

When the mighty Industrial Revolution reached Carmarthenshire with the railway, the importance of the port waned. In the 1840s the port needed help to accommodate expected increases in the export of coal, copper, tinplate, and the additional imports of iron ore, copper ore and tin generated by the industrialisation of South Wales's mining and refinery operations. The port at Llanelli was expanded to include 'New Dock' and 'Llangennech Dock' along with the introduction of a new floating 'East Dock' at Burry Port.

The ports of Llanelli and Burry Port, once less economically active than Carmarthen, slowly began taking control of the county's maritime trade. By the 1920s, compounded by an increased use of the railway networks to haul goods, Carmarthen was no longer a viable option. And its maritime era ended with the departure of its last commercial steamer in 1938.

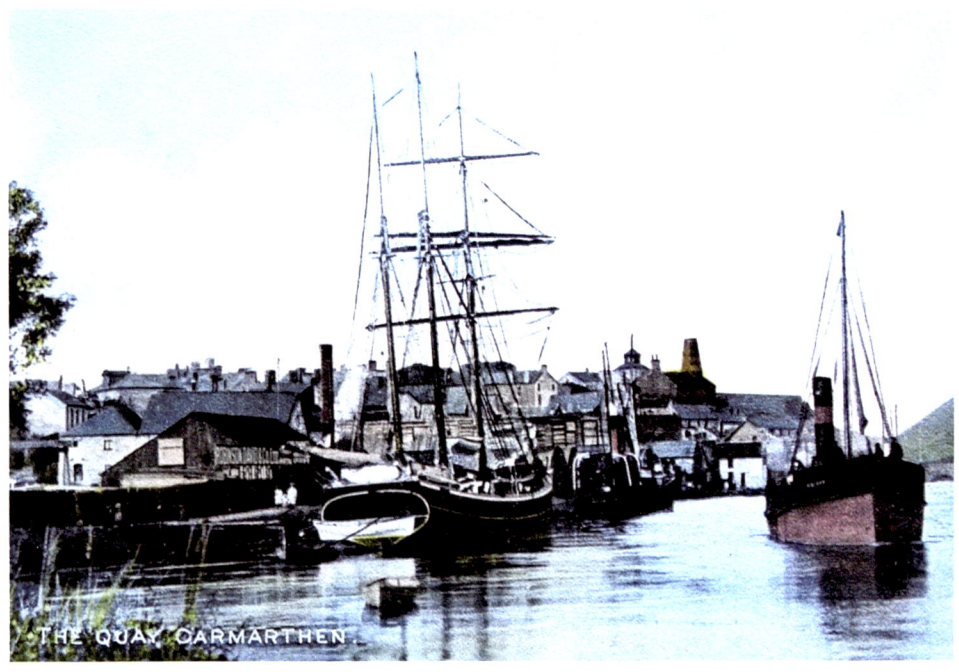

Quay, *c.* 1890. (PD)

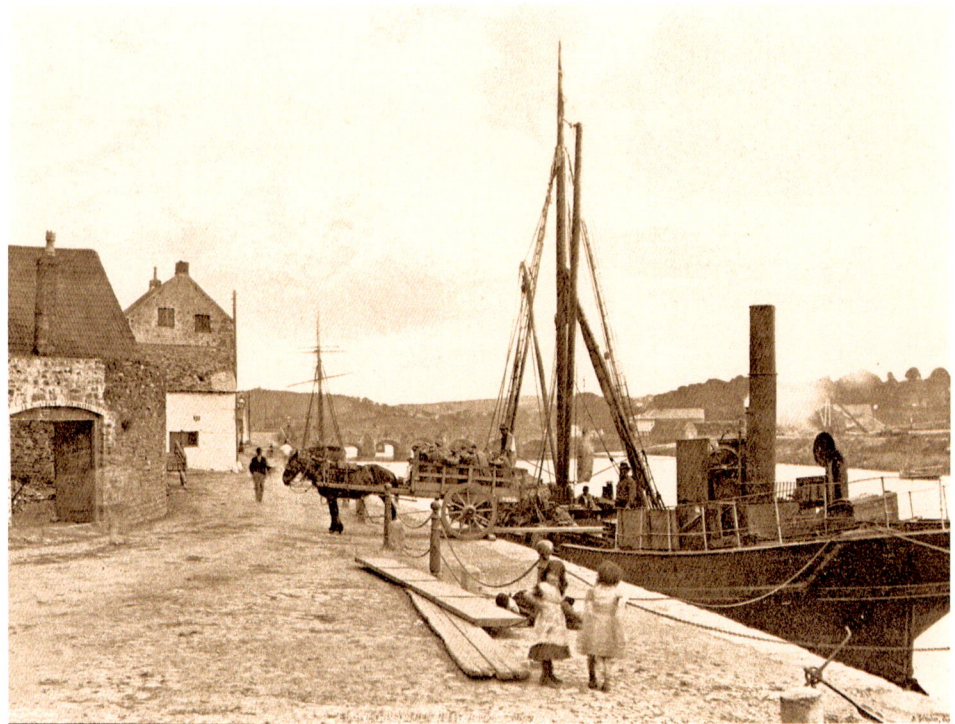

Quay, *c.* 1906. (PD)

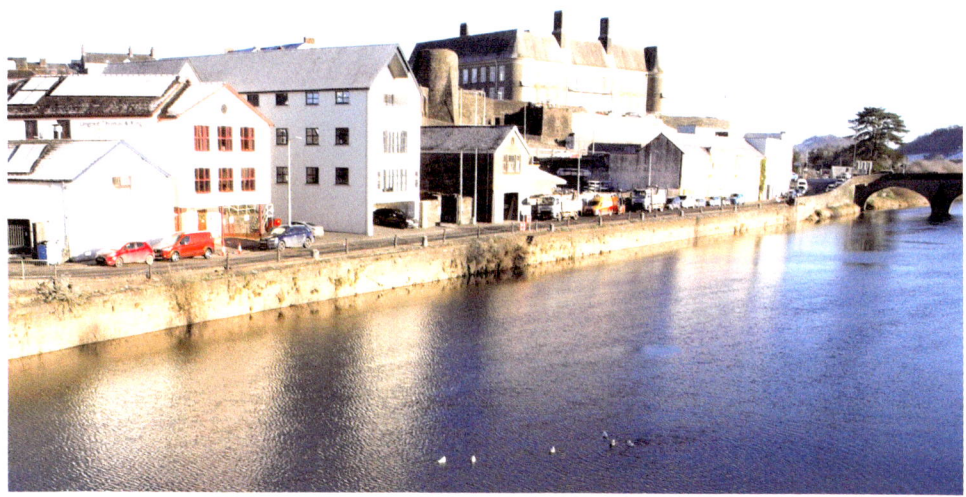

Quay, 2023.

The original stone quay wall was built during the 1550s and rebuilt and extended several times to accommodate the increasing numbers and larger types of merchant vessels docking there. Work on the new quay took place between 1807 and 1808 and the remains are visible today. A series of thirty-three fluted and tapering iron bollards with

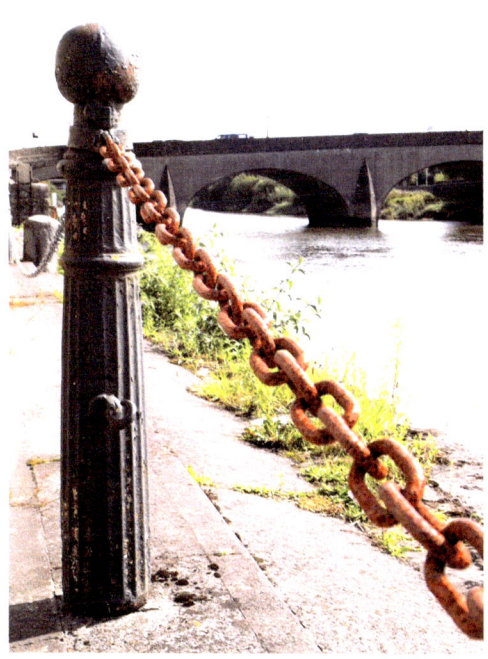

Quayside bollards.

ball finials, threaded with iron chain railings embedded in the coping of the quay's wall, are listed, as are the bollards made at the local Priory Foundry around 1860. In 1813 a slip was built near the bridge extending to Island House, opposite the end of what is now Blue Street.

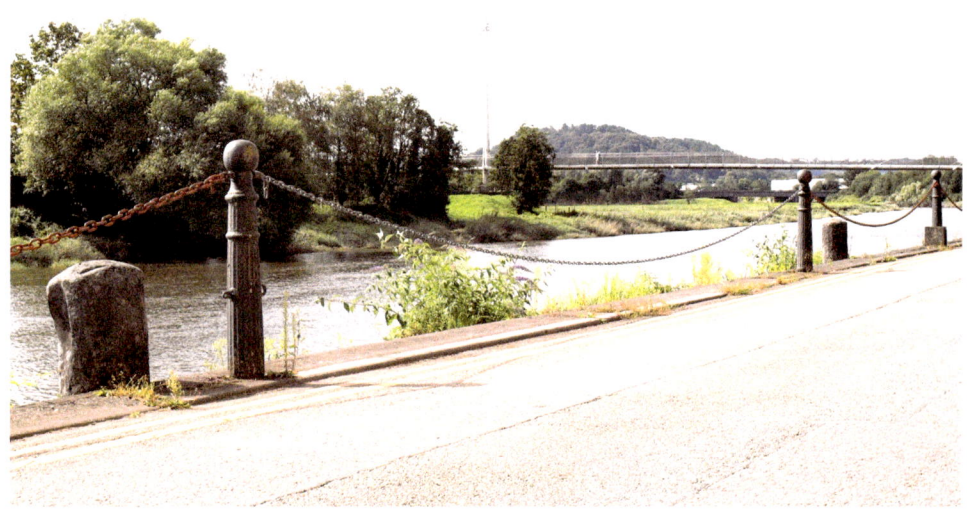

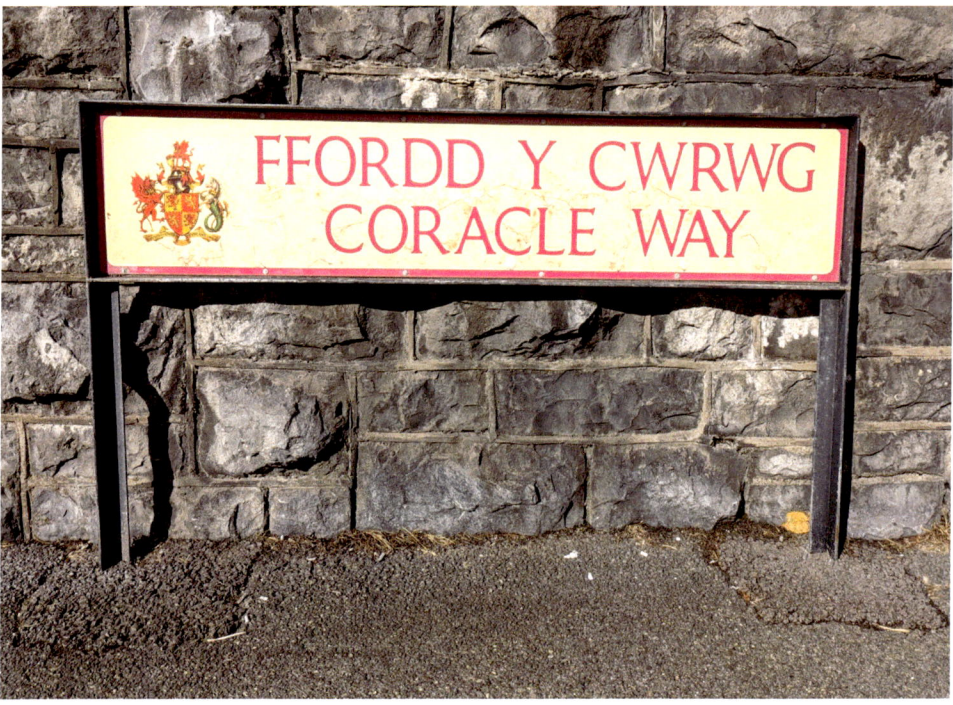

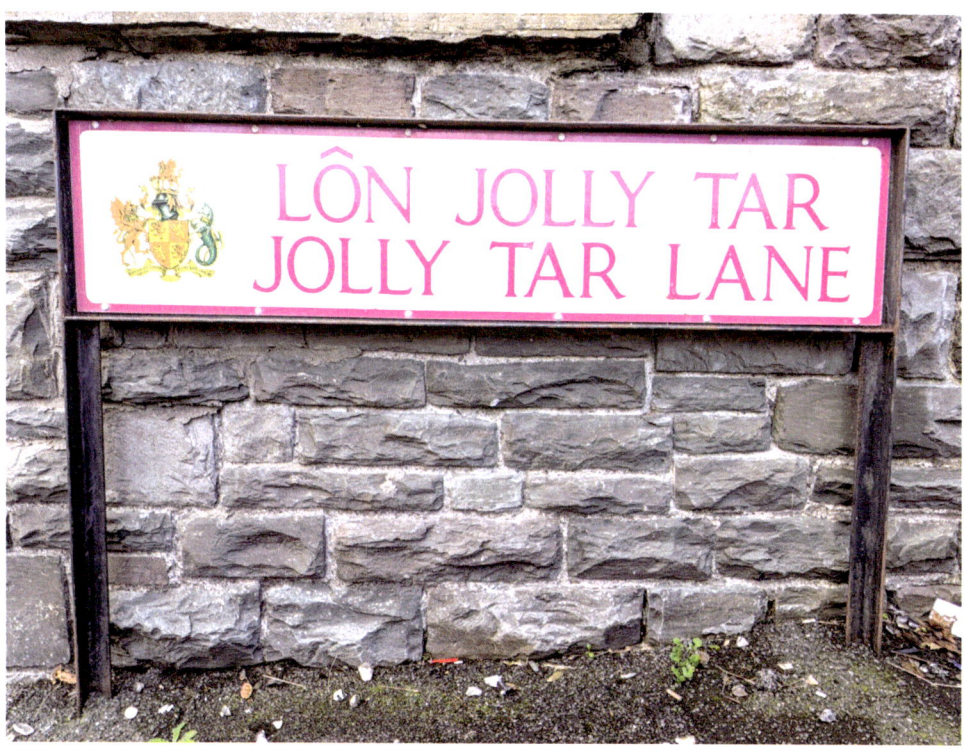

The records of the town's old street names and ale houses give an interesting insight into the town's maritime past, although most are now long gone; for example, Sailor's Ally, Nelson's Place, and Navigational Lane. At the Quay, refreshments were offered by the Hope and Anchor, the Ship Around, the Sloop, The Jolly Tar, and the Three Mariners. In Quay Street there was the Ship and Castle, in Blue Street there was the Nelson and the Shipwrights Arms, and in Red Street there was the Ship and the Jolly Sailor. Other nautically named ale houses found in the town included the Pirate, the Boat, the Anchor, the Boat and Anchor, the Ropemaker's Arms, the Lord Nelson, the Three Compasses and the Ship Inn. Among the streets that remain are Coracle Way, Jolly Tar Lane, Quay Street, The Quay, and Quay Street Bank.

2. Crime and Punishment

Since time immemorial people have broken the law, and offenders have been punished according to that law. Carmarthen's history of crime and punishment differs little from most other towns.

When the Celtic people migrated from Europe to Wales so did their European tribal justice that used forms of corporal and capital punishment to deter offenders, regulate behaviour, and punish lawbreakers.

These changes saw tribal chieftains or elders hold meetings at which an accused's guilt or innocence was decided. For more serious offences guilt or innocence was decided by undertaking an ordeal. Ordeals varied from region to region and were often defined by the local terrain, religious beliefs, and tribal customs. Most ordeals subjected the accused to a painful and/or dangerous experience.

Ordeals were based on the premise that God would help the innocent by performing a miracle on their behalf. They often included fire, applied directly or indirectly to the body, and water to scold. Other trials involved ingesting poison or fights to the death. An accused person found guilty by ordeal would then be punished. Sentences varied from forfeiture of property, title, or lands, to shunning, exile and execution. For lesser crimes offenders were ordered to pay compensation or marked by cutting, branding, or amputating body parts.

In the tenth century King Hywel 'the Good' of Deheubarth, effectively ruler of all Wales, called an assembly at Whitland, west of Carmarthen, and codified laws, parts of which were later developed and applied until the sixteenth century. The laws were very progressive, even by today's standards, with capital punishment only prescribed for a small number of crimes. Homicide was usually dealt with by the payment of compensation to the victim's family, and women's rights were recognised. In general, a man was only allowed to hit his wife if he found her with another man, and if a wife found her husband with other women three times, she could divorce him and claim half the estate.

When Edward I conquered Wales in 1283, he imposed Norman rule on the Welsh to ensure the Normans kept their power and control. Norman rule adopted several Anglo-Saxon traditions such as using constables and watchmen to keep the peace and enforce local curfews in towns and large villages. The tithing was also kept, groups of men guaranteeing each other's good behaviour, along with the hue and cry, which demanded everyone help chase and catch a criminal or face a fine.

Much of today's legal system has its roots in the Norman rule, which adopted and expanded the Saxon method of trying criminals through a court system. During trials people swore religious oaths promising to tell the truth about a person's guilt or innocence based on their knowledge of the person on trial or face God's punishment.

The Norman court system was hierarchical. Manor courts at village level were where the lord of the manor dealt with day-to-day cases. Church courts dealt with religious and moral crimes, including adultery and any crimes committed by members of the Church.

Next came the Lord's Court, which dealt with tenants, criminal cases and disputes concerning property. The next level was the Hundred Court, dealing with minor disputes that did not need to be heard by the sheriff. The Shire Court was where the sheriff heard cases of violent crime, theft, and land disputes. The highest court was the King's Court, which dealt with royal pleas and the most serious offences – murder, treason, arson, robbery, rape – along with appeals from the lower courts.

Those sentenced to prison were taken to the nearest castle and placed in the dungeon, or in the main tower. Records show that in 1275 the dungeon of Carmarthen Castle needed repair and refurbishment took place between 1287 and 1289. The earliest documentary records of prisoners being held at the castle date to 28 February 1443 when David ap Thomas was required to abide in the prison until he was able to pay the king the 1,000 marks that he owed.

Once one of the largest castles in medieval Wales, today its rubble masonry forms a stone motte, twin-towered gatehouse, a corner tower, and wall turret with short sections of curtain wall. The castle continued to serve as a local gaol until it became the county prison in 1789. Accommodation, such as it was, included a small damp cell with a mud floor and prisoners were denied furniture and lighting. Men, women, and children of

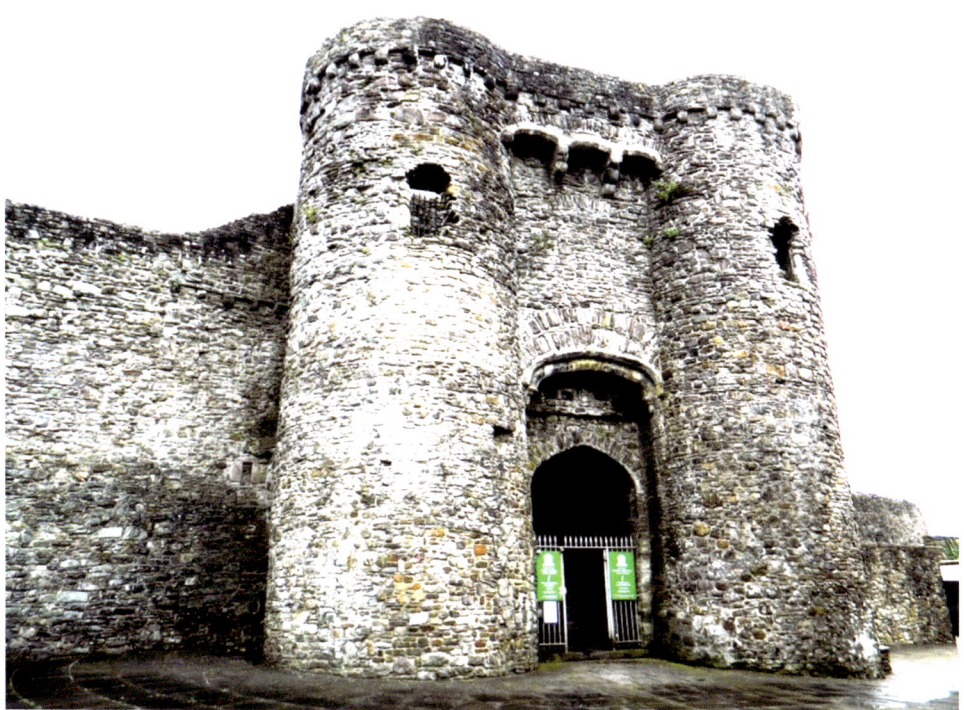

Remains of the castle.

all ages crowded together in small rooms with no heating, ventilation, or fuel. Some were subjected to routine acts of sexual abuse, and all suffered dank, damp, and cold conditions. The main condemned cell had water running down the wall. Many prisoners were never released, and died of disease, malnourishment, and hyperthermia.

Their gaolers were not salaried officials and often lived some distance away, returning only to perform menial tasks and check on the prisoners. Most were morally corrupt and had no scruples about their lack of care for the welfare or wellbeing of those in prison. Their income came via bribes, discharge fees, and other levies extorted from prisoners, family members, and friends. Often prisoners in gaol were acquitted in court, only to be detained at the whim of the gaolers until they had paid a discharge fee.

Besides the principal gaol within the castle's walls, there was the Prisoner's Gate Gaol at the town's East Gate, between King Street and Notts Square. This borough gaol was where the town's debtors were imprisoned. As in the castle gaol, conditions were grim. Sanitation was non-existent, the structure dilapidated, with squalid living conditions. Passers-by in the street below would often see illicit baskets being lowered down from the windows with appeals for food and shouts of 'Remember the Poor debtors'.

If the debtors had no family or friends to provide them with any sustenance, they were dependent upon charity, the 'Poor Law Guardians', and the mercy of others for food and medicines. This situation was commonplace throughout the United Kingdom and Europe until social change activists pursued reforms in sentencing tariffs and how prisoners were treated.

One such person was John Howard, an English philanthropist and penal reformer. During an extensive tour of British and European gaols in 1774 he visited Carmarthen and saw at first-hand the inhuman conditions experienced by prisoners and the corrupt practices of their gaolers. Howard persuaded the House of Commons to pass two Acts. The first dictated criminals should be set at liberty in open court and abolished discharge fees. The second made local justices responsible for the health of people in their gaols. Howard returned to Carmarthen fourteen years later and was appalled to find that despite the change in legislation, the conditions in both gaols had deteriorated in his absence and that corrupt gaolers were still obtaining discharge fees.

Following a meeting with freeholders, clergy and the local justices of Carmarthen, Howard sent a report to Parliament. In it he begged for a Bill to be passed ordering the construction in Carmarthen of a new single gaol to serve both the borough and county and that the existing gaols be demolished.

Parliament authorised the request and raised funds to pay for its construction. The existing castle gaol was renovated and rebuilt by one of Britain's foremost Georgian and Regency architects, John Nash. It reopened in 1792 as the County Gaol, formed by eight cells, one day room, and a yard for exercising. Prisoners spent their time either brick cleaning, cooking, sewing, clog making, on the treadwheel supplying water to the prison, stone breaking or performing general cleaning and mending activities. The old East Gate gaol had closed, but the Town Corporation argued they still needed a town gaol.

During 1869 much of the County Gaol's internal open space, along with the remains of the old castle, were reclaimed to make more prison accommodation. In 1810 a small gaol called the Roundhouse, which was also known as the borough gaol, was built on

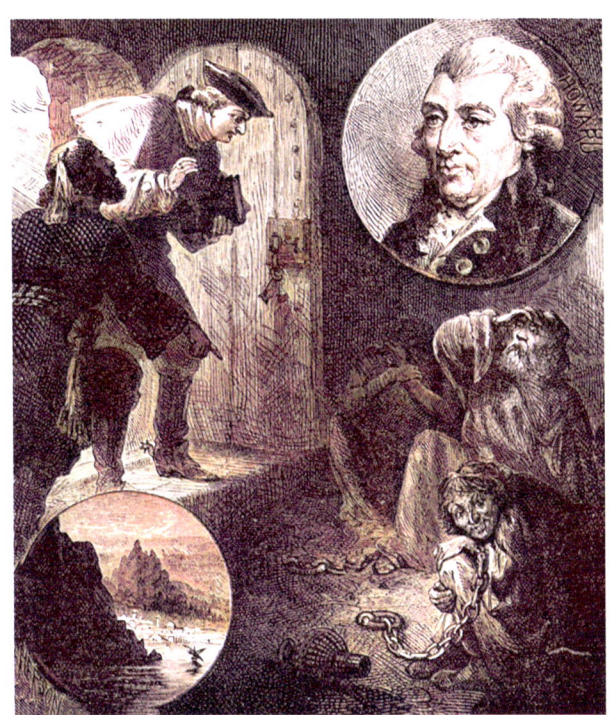

Right: John Howard. (TJHSC)

Below: New County Hall.

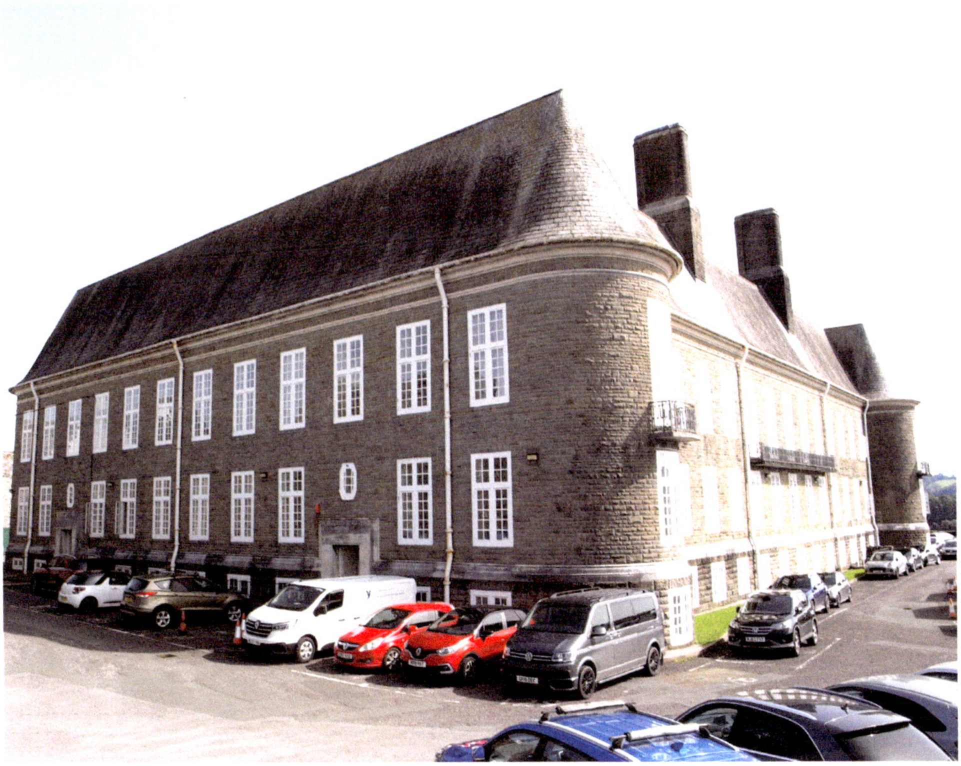

the Old Bowling Green, today the site of John Street and Cambrian Place. It only had four rooms and a small exercise yard to accommodate twelve to eighteen offenders. There was no work for the prisoners who were confined to their cells seven days a week with short periods of exercise at the gaoler's discretion. The County Gaol closed in 1922 and was demolished in the 1930s to make way for a new County Hall, which still stands today.

DID YOU KNOW?
Within the county gaol prisoners received three types of punishment. They were made to work the treadmill, using their bodyweight to turn a cylindrical drum 6 feet in diameter which would pump water from the well into tanks in the roof. Each session lasted three hours, with a five-minute break every quarter hour. The crank was another form of punishment. Prisoners were forced to turn a mechanical handle thousands of times for no reason. Prison warders today are known as 'Screws', which comes from officers tightening the crank's mechanism to make the prisoner work harder. Carmarthen gaol also ran the silent system where prisoners could eat and work together but not look at or talk to each other. The system relied on fear of punishment, using the tread, the crank or extended periods of solitary confinement.

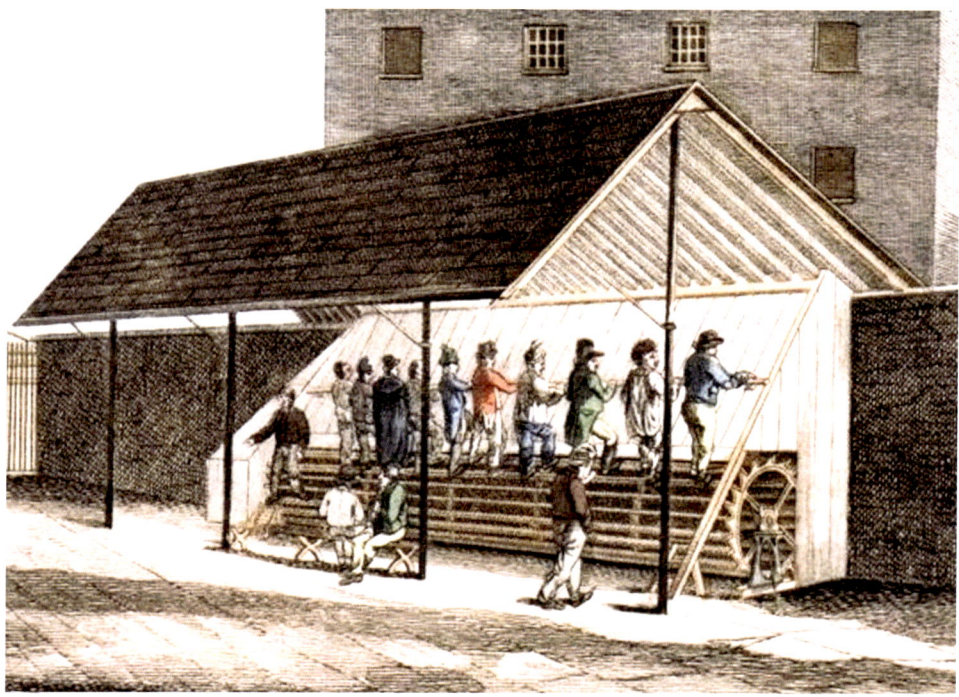

Typical prison treadwheel. (FJB)

During the seventeenth and eighteenth centuries Carmarthen had a reputation throughout Wales for being a violent town where drunkenness was prevalent, and brawling in its streets and alehouses was frequent. Despite this reputation crime rates were low, given the levels of poverty and poor housing conditions. Murder, theft, and burglary were sporadic, most offenders were debtors.

For minor offences wrongdoers were sentenced to spend time 'inconvenienced and embarrassed' in a variety of devices throughout the town. A ducking stool was located between the Little Key and the Old Water Gate during the 1690s. It was used mainly to punish disorderly women, scolds, and dishonest tradesmen. The stool was a wooden armchair made of oak. An iron band was placed around the offender's body to prevent escape and falling out during immersion.

Other punishments included the pillory, an upright post with two boards attached where apertures let the offender rest their neck and wrists. They stayed upright in an extremely uncomfortable position while passers-by ridiculed and humiliated them. Alternatively, they were placed in the equally humiliating but less uncomfortable stocks, held in a similar manner but sitting down with their ankles locked between two boards.

To maximise the offender's humiliation and tell as many people as possible what the offender had done, stocks and pillories were placed in public places such as roadsides near to town entrances and exits, church gates, market squares and other meeting places. Depending upon the crime they'd committed and their popularity, passers-by would

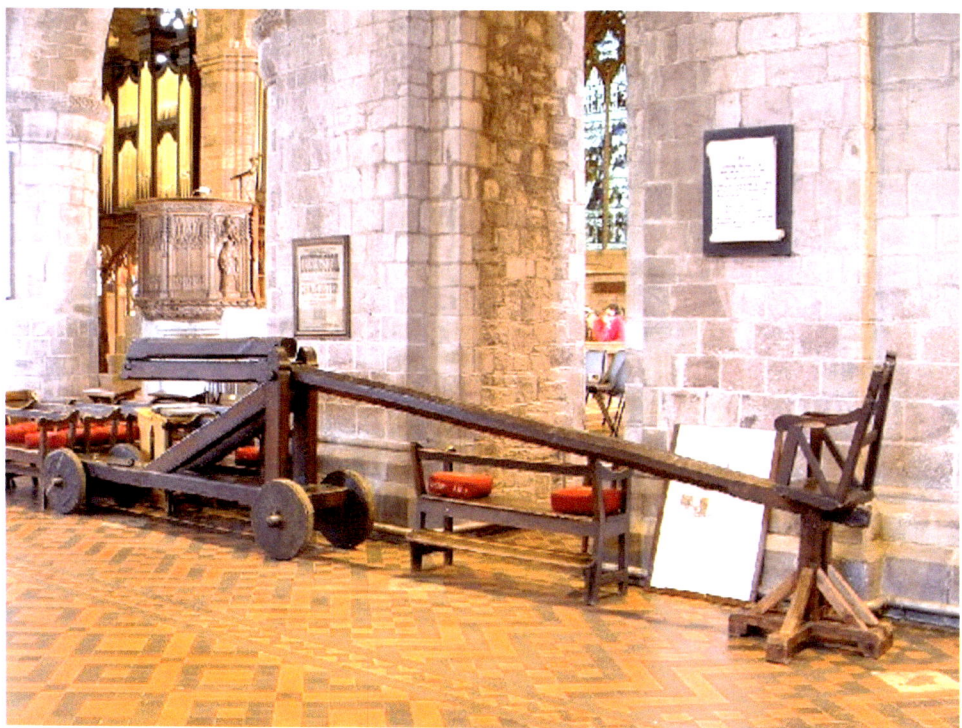

Traditional town ducking stool. (© John Phillips)

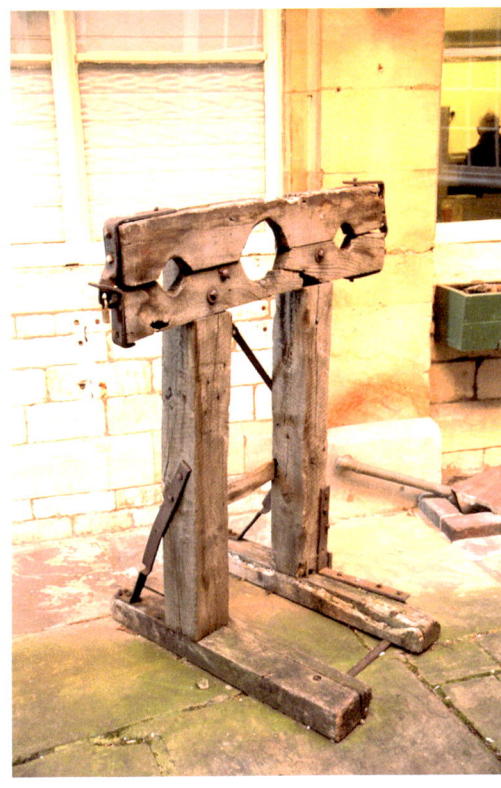

Left: Pillory. (© Richard Croft)

Below: Stocks. (© Graham Hogg)

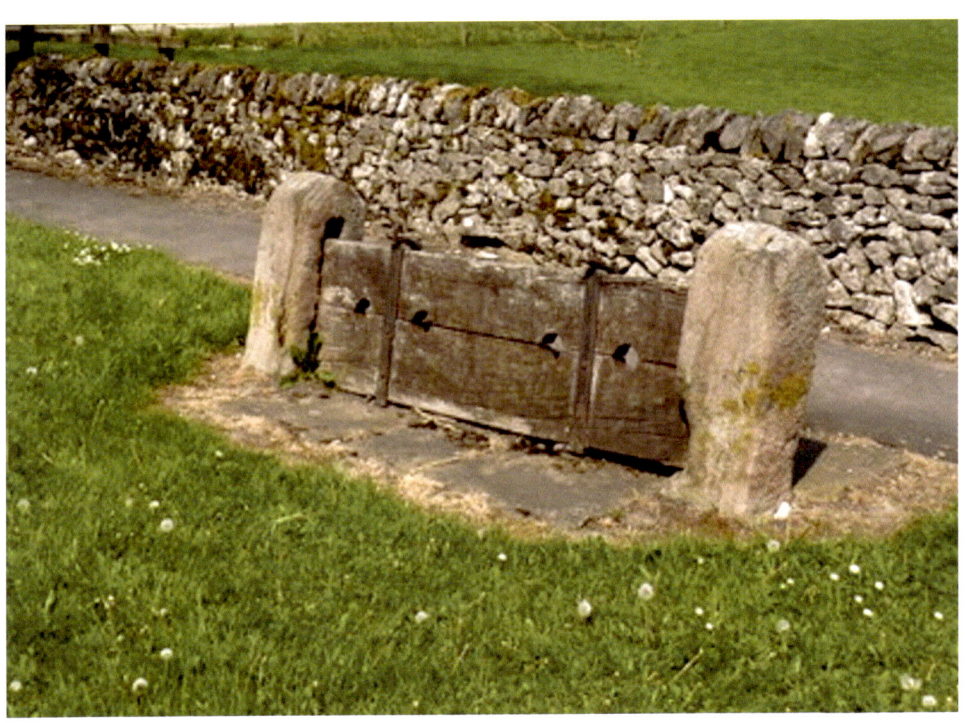

insult and throw rotten food, animal faeces, stones, or urine at them. Non-town residents would be returned to their villages and placed in local stocks or pillories.

Whipping was a common punishment for thieves, blasphemers, poachers, men, women and the insane found guilty of minor offences. Victims were tied to the end of a cart and dragged through the town; it would stop now and then so the offender could be publicly whipped. During the 1590s whipping posts were introduced as part of, or sited next to, the stocks.

The last man to stand in the pillory at Carmarthen was Thomas Evans from Gwernogle, known as Tomos Glyn Cothi. Nicknamed 'Little Priestley,' Thomas embraced the doctrines set forth by Joseph Priestley's Unitarianism and in 1786 began preaching in a chapel. He was respected by many for his liberalism, but his outspoken notions of freedom and sympathy with the French Revolutionaries brought him into conflict with the authorities.

In 1802, following information provided by one of Thomas's congregation, he was convicted of singing 'To Liberty,' an adaptation of the French 'Marseillaise' in public.

> And when upon the British shore
> The thundering guns of France shall roar,
> Vile George shall trembling stand,
> Or flee his native land.

Despite denying this, he was sentenced to two years' imprisonment and to stand in the pillory. Thomas bought a brand-new waistcoat and overcoat to wear while standing in the pillory and when a woman threw a rotten egg at him the crowd turned on her. He used his time in prison to write an English to Welsh dictionary published in 1809.

The ultimate punishment was execution and by 1723 a system known as the Bloody Code was set up in Britain, imposing the death penalty for over 200 offences. The most usual form of execution was hanging in a public place. Carmarthen gained a reputation of being the hanging town where hundreds were executed in front of crowds of thousands of people with the wealthiest paying to secure the best vantage point.

In Carmarthen executions took place on the Royal Oak Common, Johnstown, while county executions were held at Pensarn, in a field behind Babell Chapel. The field, once known as Gallows Field, was at the end of a 1-mile walk from the town, lined by spectators.

Among the infamous condemned to hang at Pensarn was Edward Higgins, who, after a lifetime of crime, eventually submitted to the hangman's noose in 1767. In 1754 Higgins was convicted of burglary and transported to the American colonies for seven years. He burgled a house and stole a large amount of money as soon as he arrived in Boston. From this and other criminal activities, he soon became wealthy enough to buy his passage home and rent a room for him, his wife and five children at the George and Dragon Hotel, Knutsford, Cheshire.

He told his friends his wealth came from the many properties he owned and that he routinely made long journeys across England and Wales to collect rents. In fact, he was a ruthless murderer, burglar, and highwayman. Higgins' crime wave paid for a large house in Cheshire, the base for his criminal enterprise until his arrest at Carmarthen for burglary at Lady Maud and Madam Bevan's home in Laugharne in the summer of 1767.

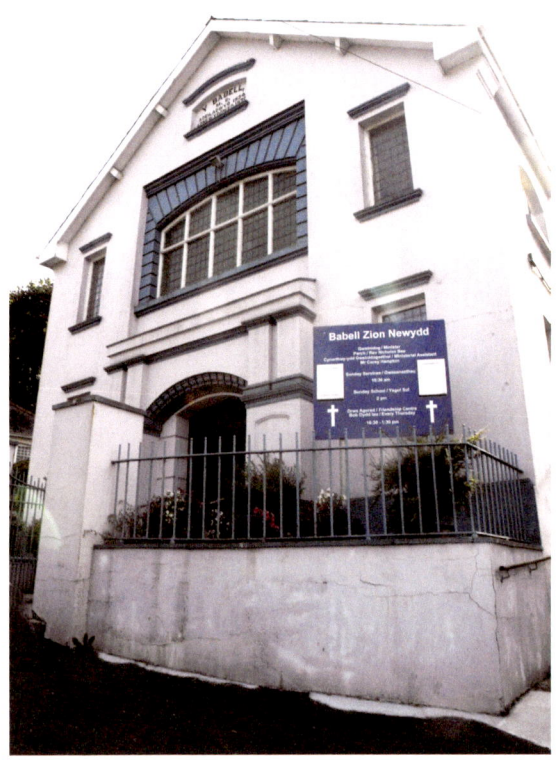

Left: Babell Chapel.

Below: Carmarthen Gaol. (PD)

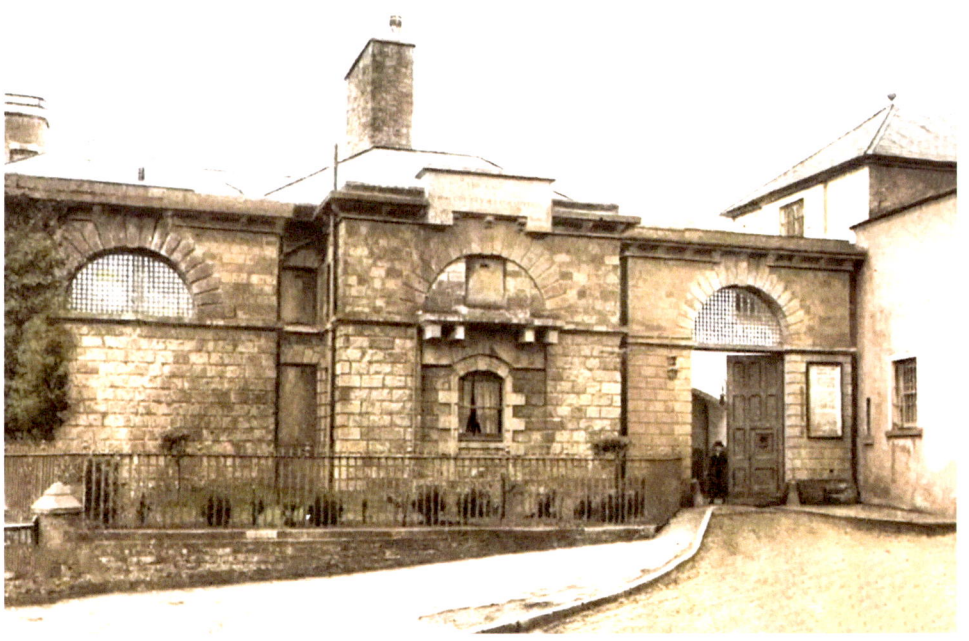

Higgins' wife and sister travelled in disguise to the sheriff's office in Carmarthen four days before Higgins was due to be hanged. They delivered a fake reprieve supposedly written by Lord Shelburne. Though he guessed it was a fake, but not wanting the death of a reprieved man on his conscience, the sheriff made inquiries. When he was satisfied, on 6 November, he told Higgins to prepare himself for execution the following morning, when he would be 'sent to eternity'.

The next dawn large crowds defied bitter cold to gather outside Carmarthen gaol and along the route to Pensarn. There was a carnival atmosphere with musicians, jugglers and other entertainers performing. Merchants sold toys depicting the hanging, along with pies and ales.

During the 1-mile walk to his death the crowd, having learned of the reprieve, constantly jeered and threatened the sheriff, demanding Higgins' release. Having reached the scaffold at Babell Hill, Higgins, with a flower in his buttonhole, addressed the sheriff saying, 'Gentlemen, now is the time to do as you please. You have my reprieve in your custody.' He prayed a short while and then declared: 'I am ready.' But as the noose was placed around his neck, he dramatically flourished a letter confessing to several crimes, including the murder of a Bristol woman and her maidservant.

The executioner kicked the stool from under Higgins, who jerked for a while before becoming motionless. The sheriff ordered Higgins' body cut down and removed to the mortuary sooner than it should have been owing to the restless nature of the crowd.

Higgins had sold his body for educational purposes to a London surgeon called Cruikshank to support his family after his death. But that was not the end of Higgins. His body had not hanged for the relevant period and at the mortuary he was still alive. It was reported that he was 'switched off' on the table.

The last hanging to take place at Pensarn was that of Rees Thomas Rees on 19 April 1817. Rees, a lay preacher, was convicted of poisoning his pregnant sweetheart Elizabeth Jones. Following his execution new gallows were built inside the front wall of the county gaol facing Spilman Street.

William Baines was the first man to be hanged on the new site on 23 May 1818. He was an engraver convicted of forging and uttering forged Bank of England notes. His execution drew a crowd of over 10,000 people eager to see the spectacle. The hanging took place on a raised platform and didn't disappoint the crowd. First, they saw Baines fail to be hanged when the trapdoor refused to open. Despite pleading for his life on the grounds he could not be punished twice for the same offence the second time worked and proved fatal.

Of note is the curious case in 1788 of the hangman who hanged himself. Barely twenty years old, the hangman had been found guilty of breaking into a house during daylight hours and stealing goods from within. It was reported he was tried three times for the offence, eventually being found guilty and convicted. Thirty minutes after being sentenced to death he hanged himself in the gaol.

The last public hanging took place on 29 September 1829. David Evans was executed for butchering his pregnant girlfriend Hannah Davies with a billhook. Like Baines, he was hanged twice when the first attempt failed. The carpenter did not tighten the hook into the beam or insert the bolts holding the beam to the uprights properly during the gallows' construction. A surprised Evans landed on his feet. Like Baines his plea that he had been hanged once and could not be hanged twice for the same offence failed and he was executed at the second attempt.

From this point hangings took place privately inside the gaol. The gaol raised a 4 by 8 inches black flag confirming prisoner execution, followed by the attaching of a notification to the outside of the prison gates, also confirming the execution had taken place. Sailor David Evans was the last person executed at the gaol on 29 November 1894 for the murder of his sister-in-law Mary Evans, who he suffocated in her bed.

DID YOU KNOW?
The 12-foot gates to the prison mysteriously disappeared after its closure in 1922 and for seventy years their whereabouts remained unknown until their arrival at Carmarthen Museum, where they are today. The last governor of the prison, Captain John Nicholas, had them rehung at his country home of Maes Teilo, Llandeilo. When it became a nursing home, the gates returned once more to hang in Carmarthen.

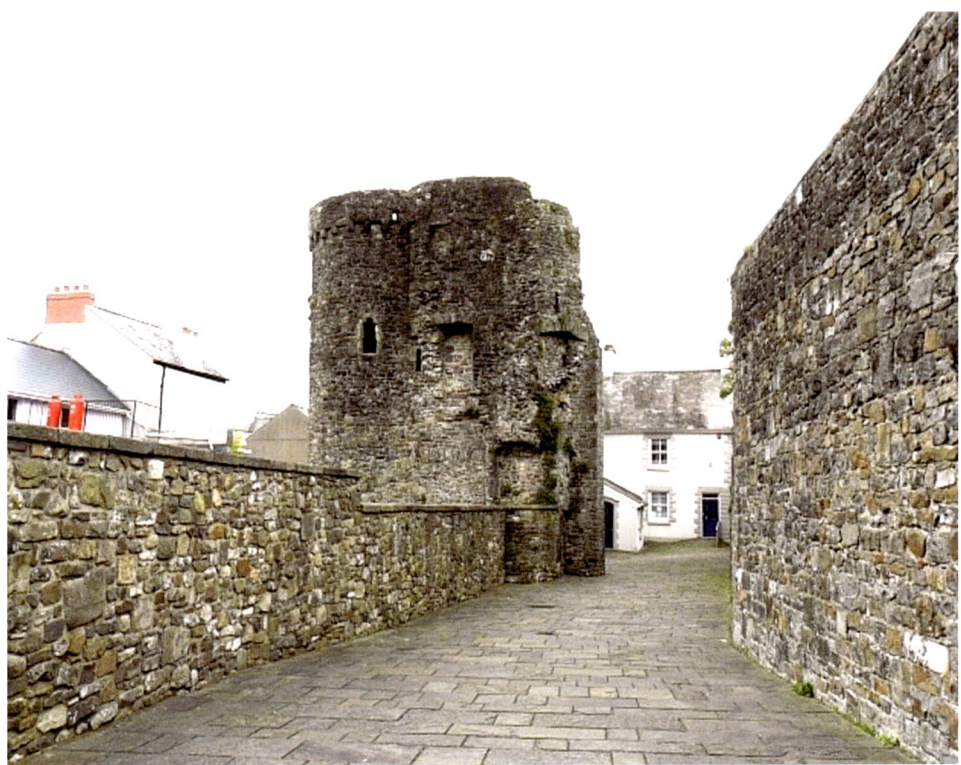

Gaol wall and old police station. (© Rose and Trev Clough)

The town's most horrific spectacle occurred in 1555 and attracted thousands from around the county when the Bishop of Saint David's, Robert Ferrar, was burnt alive at the market cross in what is now Nott Square. While studying at Oxford, Ferrar came under the influence of the teachings of the Protestant Reformation movement, in particular Martin Luther and William Tyndale. Cardinal Wolsey investigated claims of heresy and Ferrar was imprisoned twice for selling Protestant books but allowed to finish his education.

In 1549 he was appointed Bishop of St Davids, but came into conflict with his parishioners because he was married with children and had an over-zealous preaching style. He was summoned to London by Queen Mary I in September 1553. The staunchly Catholic queen, known as Bloody Mary, refused to recognise the legality of Ferrar's marriage and his Protestant views and imprisoned him. Refusing to recant, he was sent from London to Carmarthen and placed on trial for heresy at the Consistory Court in St Peter's Church. Inevitably he was found guilty and burned at the stake on 30 March 1555, one of about 300 Protestants who suffered the same fate during Mary's reign. Today, a stone plaque marks the spot where he died a martyr's death for his convictions.

DID YOU KNOW?
Robert Ferrar was not the only clergyman executed in Carmarthen. In 1633 a rotund priest, Father Arthur, also referred to as 'the Fat Irishman', was hanged, drawn, and quartered for cursing the king and conspiring to cause his death. He was taken to Pensarn, where the gruesome feat took place.

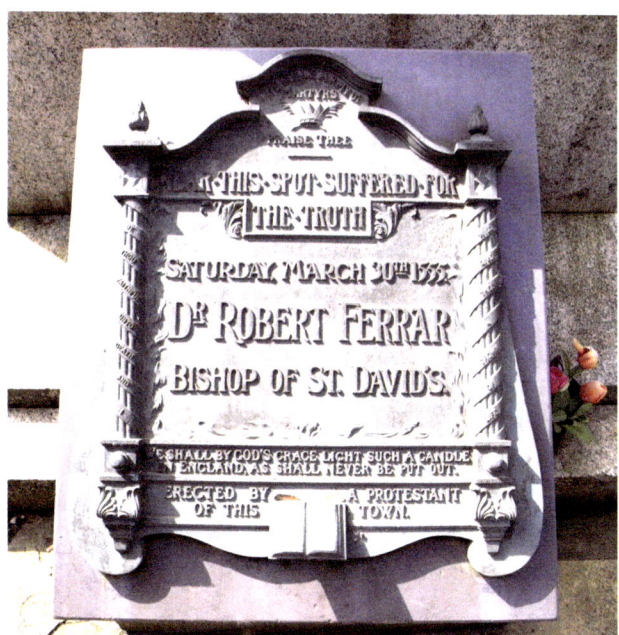

Nott Square monument.

3. Churches and Chapels

The religious history of Carmarthen is a complicated and colourful affair full of radical characters, fascinating deeds, and incredible acts of faith that occasionally resulted in expulsion, incarceration, and martyrdom. Today most of the town's religious buildings no longer exist or are not in service, either destroyed, redeveloped, rebuilt, or refurbished, leaving little evidence of the might and power, influence, and importance that religion once played in the daily lives of the town's residents. Despite this, many hundreds of the town's people still worship at chapels or churches, and the mayor's service is held annually in one of them.

Within the remaining buildings, structures and memorials are some of the town's best-kept secrets. Forgotten tales and facts about the individuals and occasions that have shaped the religious history of the town, county, Wales and beyond.

Following the Normans' arrival and settlement, Carmarthen originally existed as two towns and was noted throughout the medieval era for its monastic houses and schools. The old town originally consisted of around a hundred households built on the site of the old Roman town. It housed the Benedictine Priory of Saint Peter, later replaced by the Augustinian Priory of Saint John the Evangelist and St Teulyddog. It was one of the wealthiest institutions in Wales, and ran three watermills powered by the Gwili, a tributary of the River Tywi. Near the Glangwili Hospital, you can find part of a medieval leat that supplied water to the mills. Today the gatehouse's arched entrance and a portion of the precinct wall at the south-west corner of the town's Parc Hinds recreation area are all that's left of the priory. The rest now house four homes. The church, chapter house and foundations of the prior's quarters were uncovered during excavations in 1979, together with pieces of stained glass and medieval glazed tiles.

The new town was home to a Franciscan friary founded around 1270. It was the largest Greyfriars in Britain outside of London and covered a 5-acre site, now home to Greyfriars Shopping Centre, the former Wilko's store, and Merlin's Walk. The Greyfriars site included a church, chambers, kitchen, brewery and a buttery. The friary became a popular burial site, and many notable Welsh and English people were interned there, among them Sir Rhys ap Thomas, Welsh bard Tudur Aled, and Edmund Tudor, father of King Henry VII and founder of the Tudor dynasty.

St Peter's Church is the oldest in the county, and one of the largest parish churches in Wales. Originally a simple timber church built on the site of a first-century Roman gateway to the civitas capital of the Demetae. Today it stands as an impressive stone building that has been at the centre of the town's civic, religious and social affairs for over 1,500 years. Now the church, a Grade I listed building, is the last survivor of several associated with the monastery, once standing within the walls of the old Roman town of Moridunum. A link to this era can be seen in the porch where a Roman altar stone stands.

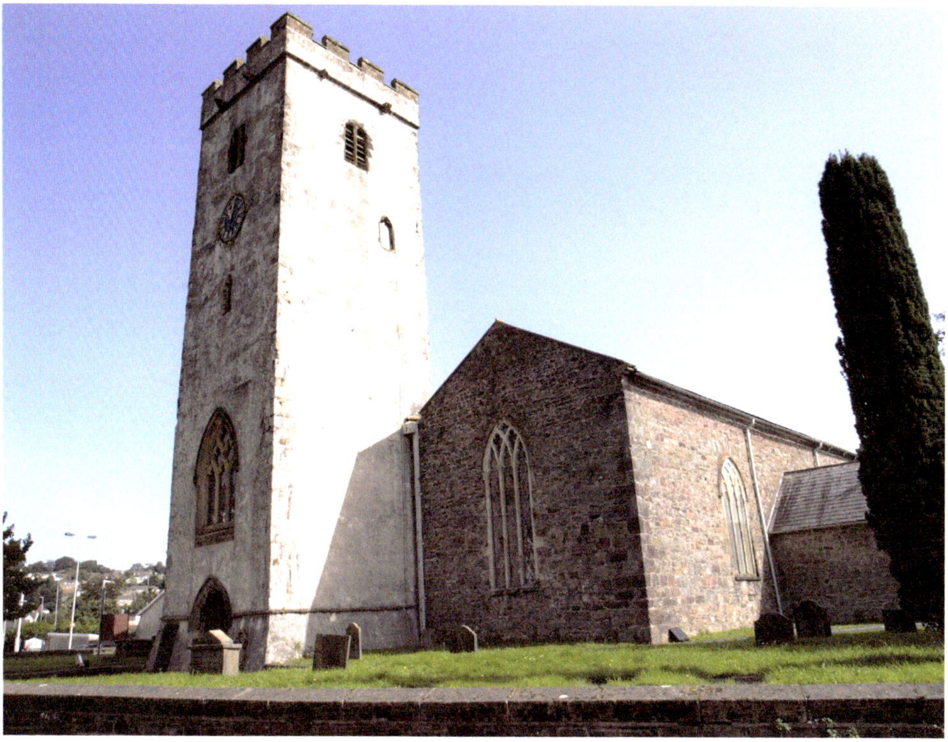

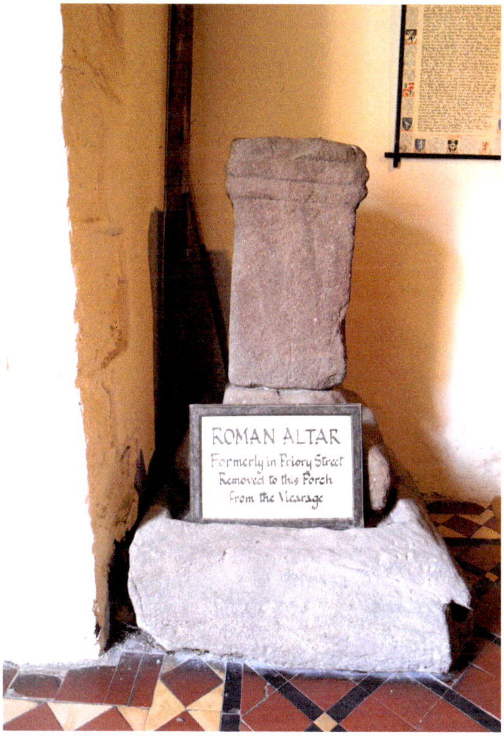

Above: St Peter's.

Right: Roman altar stone.

An unusual and interesting feature of the church is its circular graveyard. A common feature of Celtic graveyards, it suggests the site originally dates to the sixth century and possibly earlier, as Christian sites of worship were often built on existing pagan sites. There is also some evidence that an earlier ancient Celtic church, St Teulyddog's, stood nearer the river below Priory Street, later absorbed by the town's priory when St Peter's became the parish church.

Its recorded history dates from 1107 when Henry I gave it to Battle Abbey, Sussex. Battle Abbey controlled the church until it was transferred to the Bishop of St Davids. In 1125 Bishop Bernard of St Davids gave its control to the Carmarthen Priory, who oversaw it throughout the medieval period.

The tower, nave and chancel were built on the original foundations during the thirteenth century, while the south aisle and porch were added during the fourteenth century. On the north side of the chancel wall, beneath a memorial to the dead of the two world wars and just above floor level, is the church's oldest relic, a stone slab carved with an unknown figure. This is believed to be part of the earlier church. The battlements were renewed in 1776 and a new roof and plaster ceiling were added in 1785 using materials sourced from the ruins of the priory. Five years later, this ceiling was condemned, removed and replaced by the present wooden beams and in 1796 the organ was added. The tower is rendered in lime, a traditional facing for church buildings in Wales from medieval times to the nineteenth century and holds eight bells: four original bells cast in 1722, and four new bells added in 1904 along with the current clock.

During the sixteenth century, a 'Consistory Court' (a court for administering the church's own legal system) was set up and held in the church. In 1555 the Bishop of

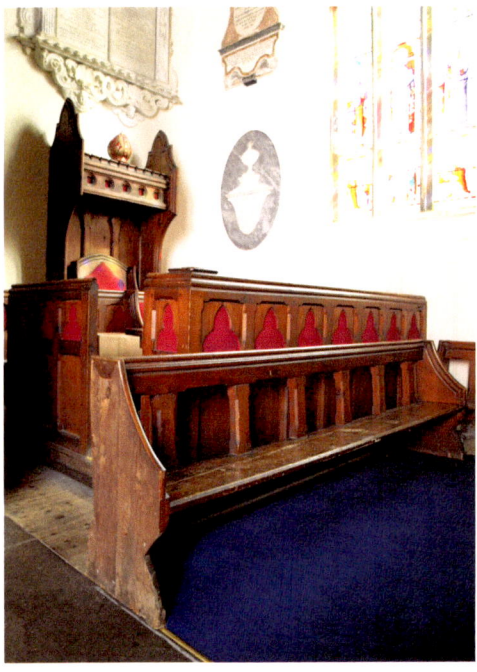

The Consistory Court.

Saint Davids, Robert Ferrar, was tried at St Peter's for heresy before being burned at the stake in the town's marketplace. The Consistory Court can still be seen in the south aisle, where a memorial to Bishop Ferrar stands.

There are many historic memorials and monuments inside the church dating from the seventeenth to nineteenth centuries and a thirteenth-century coffin lid are on display. In the churchyard some of the town's more notable characters are buried, including the tomb of General Sir William Nott (1782–1845), a veteran of campaigns in Afghanistan and India. Sir William's father famously owned an inn at Carmarthen with a sign outside the entrance saying, 'Come in, eat, drink, be merry and pay Nott'!

The most famous memorial is the tomb of Sir Rhys ap Thomas. A courageous warrior, and one of Wales's most outstanding personalities of his era, Rhys led an army from west Wales to fight for Richard III but switched sides to support Henry Tudor. There's a strong tradition, supported by a contemporary bardic poem, that it was Rhys himself who 'killed the boar (Richard) and cleaved his head' at the Battle of Bosworth. Before that epic battle and in uprisings that followed, Rhys played a key role in Henry Tudor's victory and defence of his throne. Had he not changed his allegiance the Tudor dynasty might never have happened, and British history would have run a different course. He was rewarded with vast estates for his services and later made a Knight of the Garter. His tomb was originally in the friary but following its dissolution in 1538 it was moved to St Peter's Church.

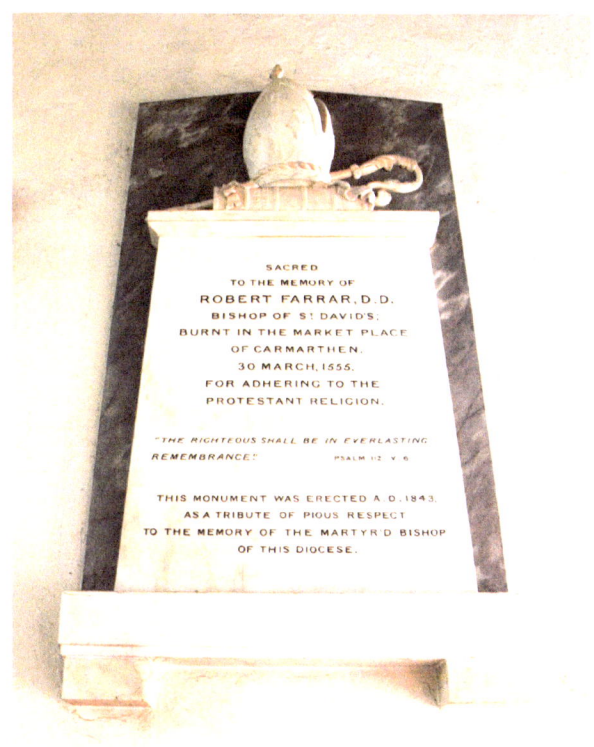

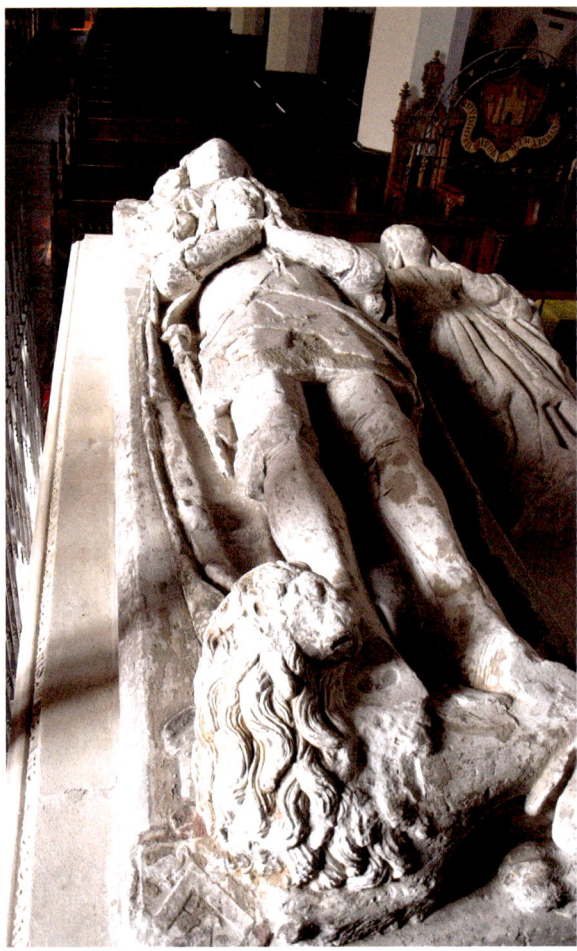

Tomb of Sir Rhys ap Thomas.

DID YOU KNOW?
For several centuries it was customary for the mayor and Corporation to attend the church in their official capacity on Christmas day. The old Tudor Sword of State and maces were carried before the mayor as he made his way to the mayor's chapel in the north transept until 1836 when the seats were removed. Today an exquisitely carved mayoral chair with worked iron rest for the sword and maces, kept in the mayor's parlour, can be seen in the transept.

Baptist Chapel, Lammas Street.

Itinerant Nonconformist preachers first visited the town in 1650 and small congregations soon formed. Following King Charles II's restoration of the monarchy in 1660 worshipers faced oppression, persecution and suppression. Congregations went into hiding and many individuals were imprisoned for their beliefs. Despite this, Nonconformists continued to meet secretly in the countryside while others held covert meetings in a storehouse on the quayside.

Among their leaders was Carmarthen-born Stephen Hughes. Hughes, the son of a silk trader who was Mayor of Carmarthen, was a great influencer and powerful preacher who became known as 'the Apostle of Carmarthenshire'. In 1667 Hughes was excommunicated for ministering in a 'dissenting conventicle at Llansteffan' on the Tywi estuary. Later, in 1674, he was arrested for committing acts recorded as 'to the prejudice of his health and hazard of his life' and imprisoned in Carmarthen gaol. A number of independent chapels in Carmarthen town and the county, and still in use today, trace their foundation back to Stephen Hughes.

Following the religious persecution that ensued from the reign of Charles II, Hughes re-established the Nonconformist faith in Carmarthen. He translated and published several books in Welsh, including a cheap edition of the Bible. Hughes collaborated with other notable Puritans to translate and publish *Pilgrim's Progress* in 1688. The importance of this work for Welsh Christianity was enormous, ensuring that Puritanism could widely use the Welsh language in its literature and education.

The congregation met in Heol y Prior (Prior Street), known locally as 'The Old Meeting House'. In 1726, the church moved to Capel Heol Awst (Lammas Street), where it was enlarged in 1802 and in 1826 reconfigured to become the building we see today, capable of seating 1,000 people. The Methodist chapel in Heol Dŵr (Water Street) also has a similar number of pews.

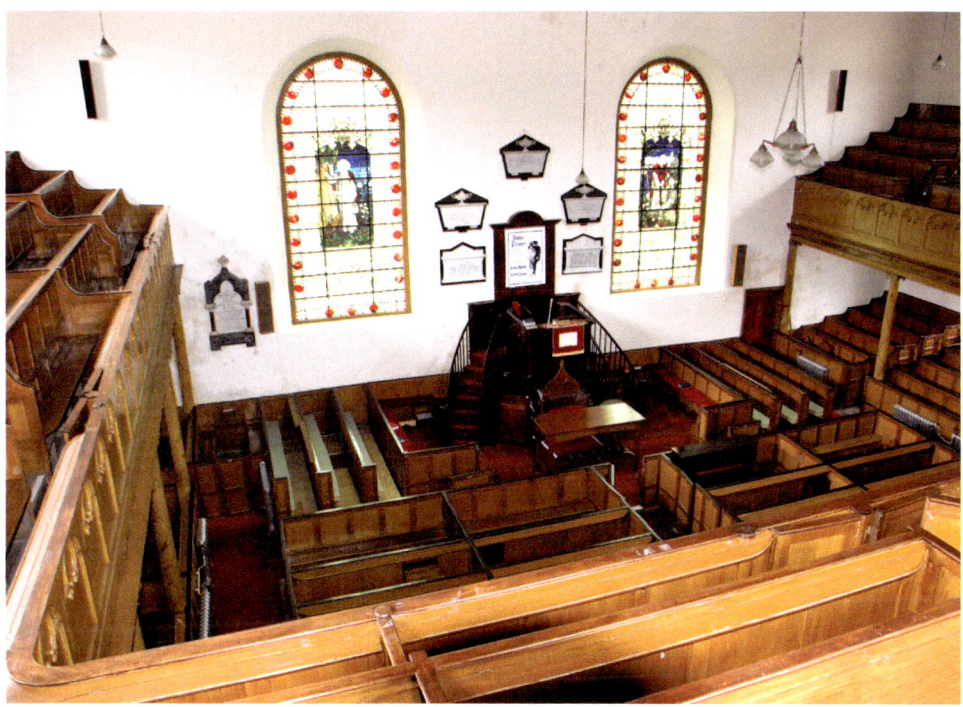

Independent Welsh Chapel. (GeraintTudur2)

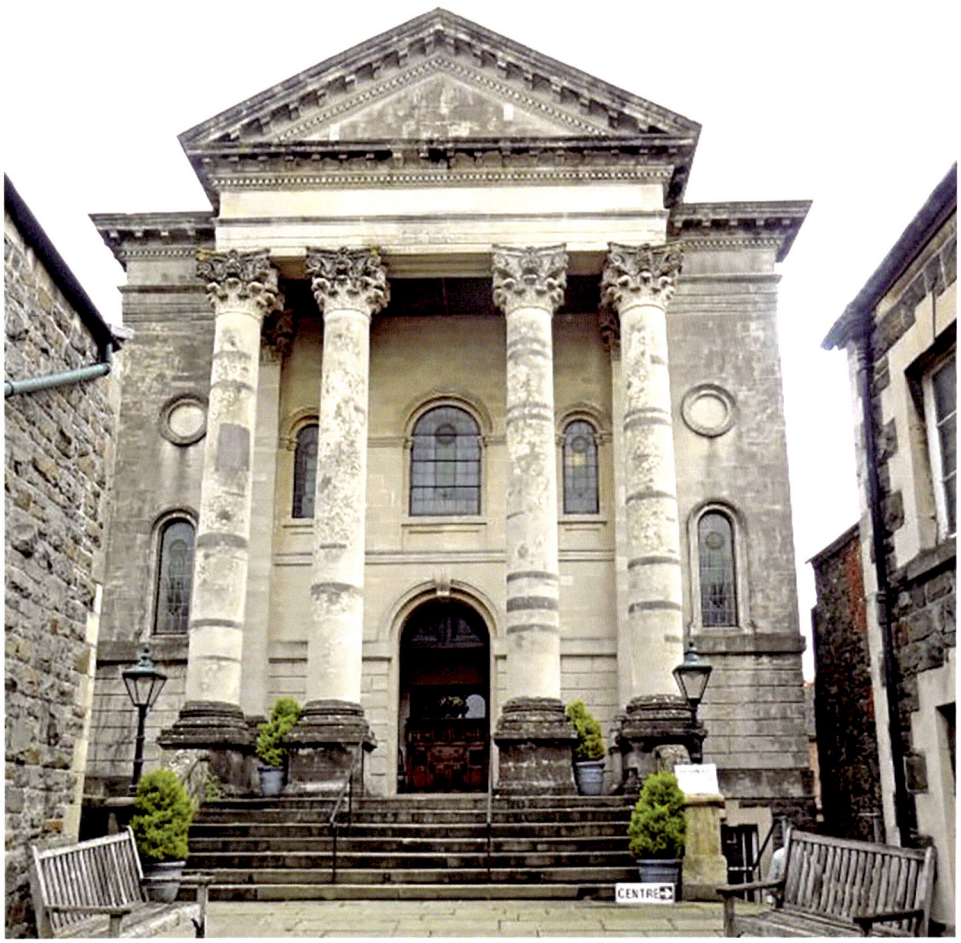

English Baptist Church.

In Dark Gate, Lammas Street, set back from the road in a courtyard where the Black Horse Inn previously stood, is the English Baptist Church. It is an imposing building with a temple-style façade built from Bath stone with wide stone steps leading to the entrance. A single raked gallery is within, and behind this an arch with painted foliage and fluted decoration. The edge of the gallery is bound by a cast-iron band and supported by cast-iron columns. Lower parts of the walls are panelled, and uniquely the original furnishings are still in place. A purpose-built gallery houses the organ, which was not installed until 1887.

The church has been associated with many prominent figures, most notably Dr Gwilym Davies (1879–1955) the pioneer of social service in Wales. Davies was a Baptist minister who dedicated his life to supporting the work of the League of Nations and its successor, the United Nations, and was a leading figure in the founding of the United Nations Educational, Scientific and Cultural Organization. He also set up the Annual World

Wireless Message to Children in 1922, and was the first person to broadcast in Welsh, on St David's Day 1923. A blue plaque commemorates his association with the church.

There have been several Baptist chapels in Carmarthen. While the present chapel building of Penuel, Priory Street, only dates to 1910, it is sited on the oldest remaining location. Originally constructed in 1786, it has been enlarged four times since then and could hold a congregation of 800 people.

Its construction came in the wake of religious discord that caused the congregation to split during the late eighteenth century. The conformist members continued to worship at Chapel Yard while the Nonconformists bought land at Parc y Siop where they built Penuel Chapel. The Baptist Association openly refused to recognise the Nonconformist Penuel Chapel congregation along with eleven other Nonconformist congregations in the 'Neighbourhood,' resulting in their expulsion from the association in 1799.

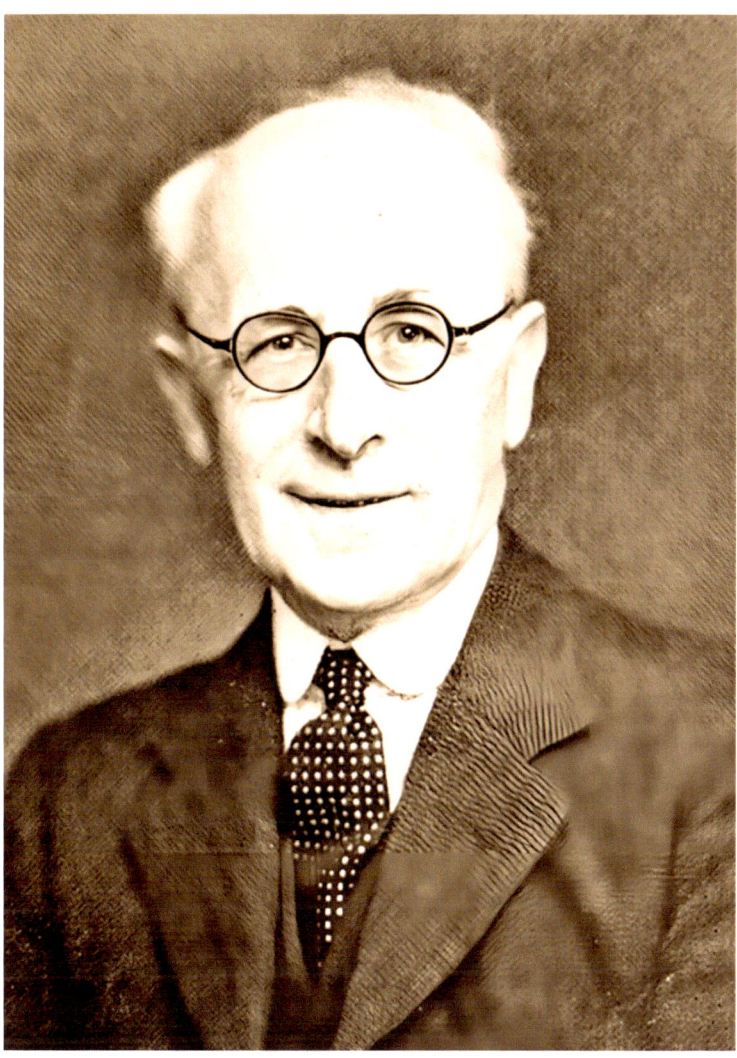

Dr Gwilym-Davies.
(PD)

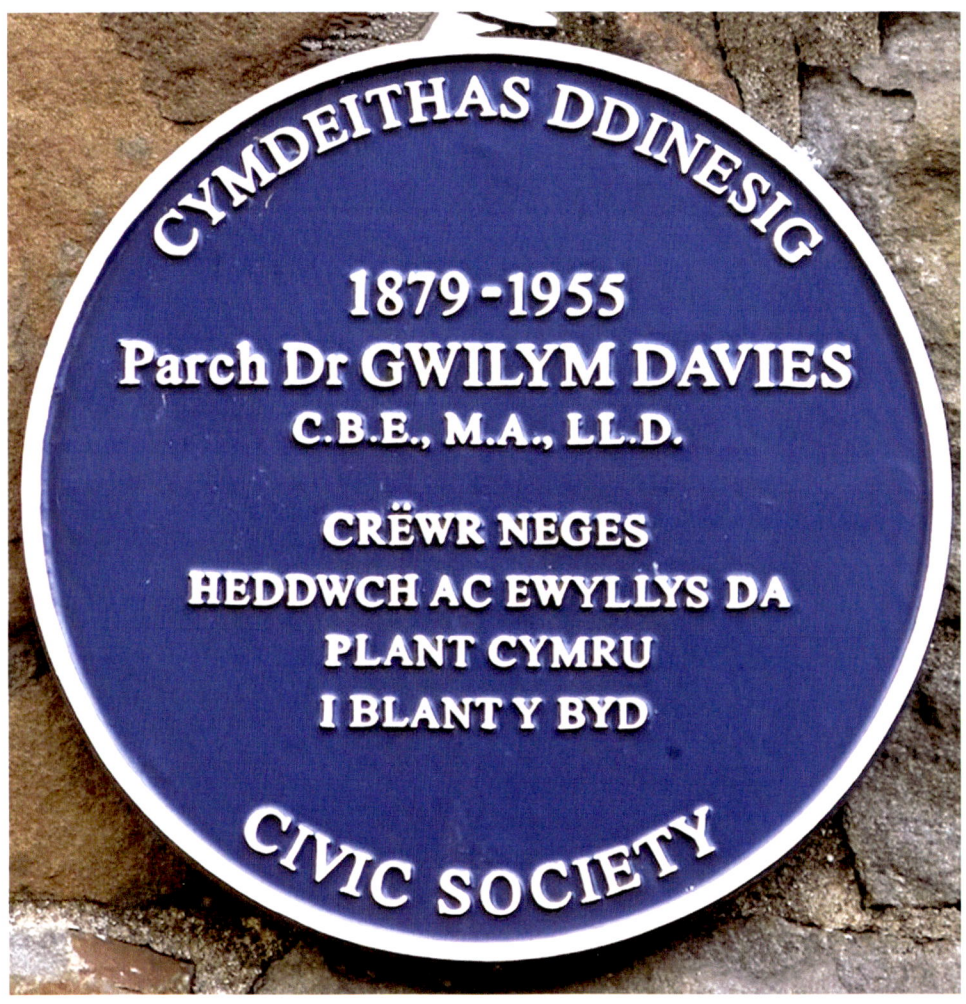

CYMDEITHAS DDINESIG

1879-1955
Parch Dr GWILYM DAVIES
C.B.E., M.A., LL.D.

CRËWR NEGES
HEDDWCH AC EWYLLYS DA
PLANT CYMRU
I BLANT Y BYD

CIVIC SOCIETY

Revd Morgan John Rhys is by far the most interesting and controversial of the many Baptist ministers to preach at Penuel Chapel. He was a distinguished Welsh radical evangelical who preached the principles of the French Revolution, condemned slavery, and championed the reform of Parliament, earning him the title 'The Welsh Baptist Hero of Civil and Religious Liberty of the Eighteenth Century'. Rhys introduced a system of Sunday schools in Wales, and the teaching of English in day schools through the Welsh language. He was also a noted poet and wrote hymns still sung today, penning twenty-two in Carmarthen during 1760.

Along with the Welsh Independent Churches, Calvinistic Methodism is a purely Welsh denomination, and the only one to make use of the title Calvinistic (after the founder John Calvin) in its name. The Calvinistic Methodists began worshipping in Carmarthen during the middle of the eighteenth century, meeting in a house in Goose Street (now St Catherine Street). Peter Williams, a graduate of Carmarthen Grammar School and a prominent leader of the Welsh Methodist movement, constructed a chapel in the garden

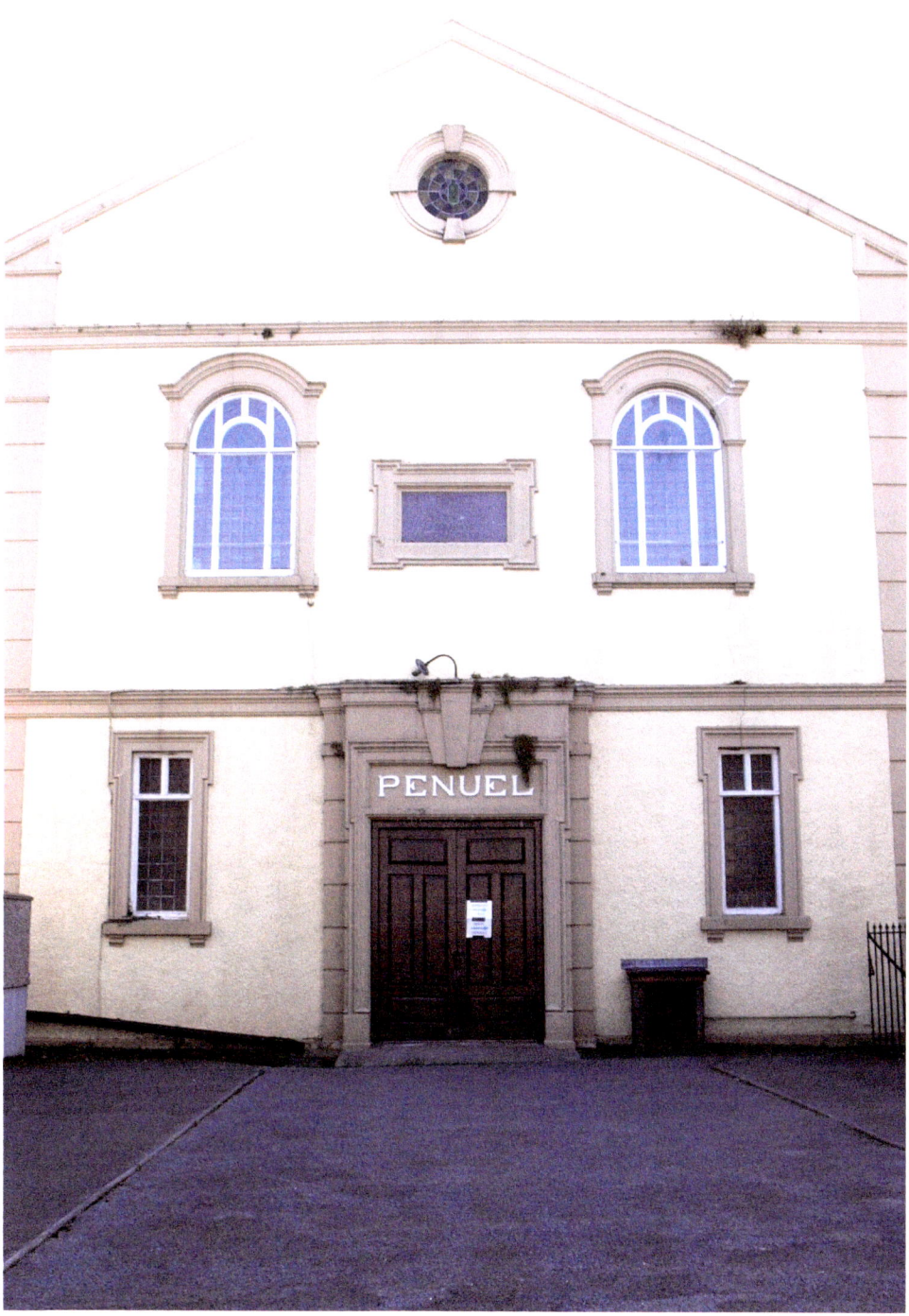

Penuel Chapel.

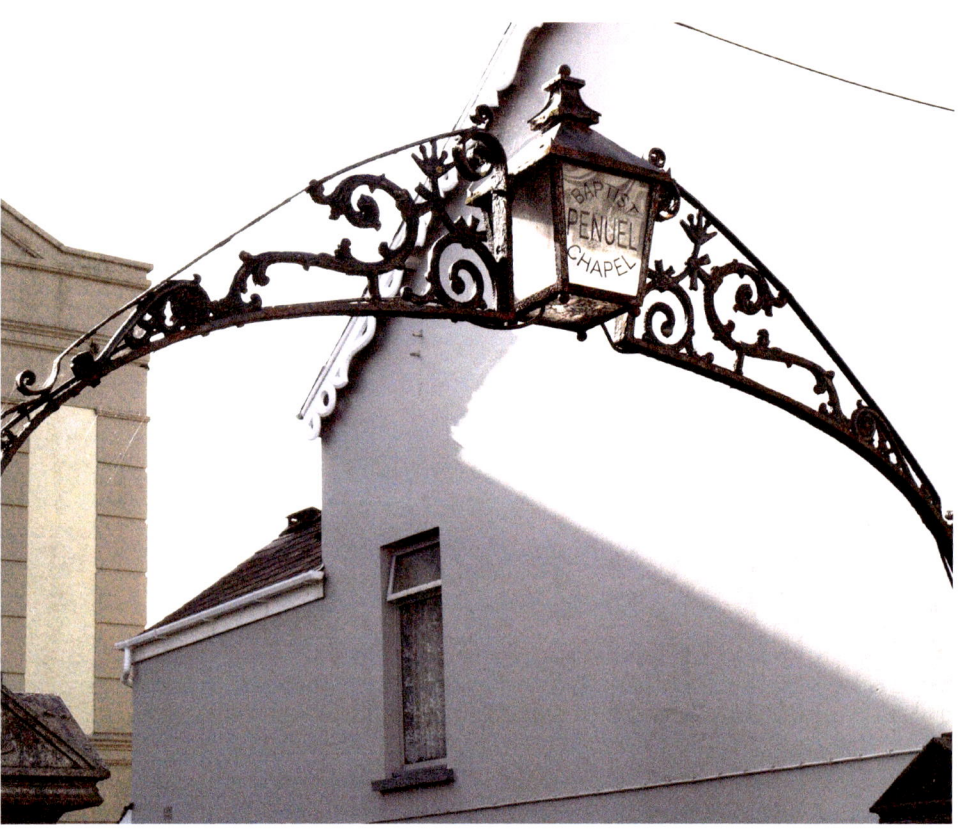

of his house in Water Street (Heol Dŵr). In 1771, Williams had a second chapel built behind the first, converting the former into a private dwelling for himself.

John Wesley, the famous Methodist leader, visited Carmarthen no less than twenty times between 1763 and 1790, during his travels on horseback to west Wales and on to Ireland. He preached on the Castle Green, in Peter Williams' chapel and in the marketplace (now Nott Square) 'to the largest congregation I ever saw in Wales' he said.

Peter Williams is renowned for publishing the first Welsh-language Bible in Wales, which included commentaries, printed by John Ross in 1770 in Carmarthen. It sold by the tens of thousands. He also translated a hymn by the great Carmarthenshire hymnist William Williams, Pantycelyn. It's commonly known as the 'Bread of Heaven' hymn sung by Welsh rugby supporters. Williams was expelled by the Methodist Association in 1791 because of his heretical views about the Trinity. Keeping the chapel, he forced the conventional Methodists to meet in Friars Park until his death in 1796. They then bought the chapel from his widow and recommenced worship the following year. Having demolished the second chapel in 1813, the society built the chapel that stands today. In 1815, they bought Williams' home, the site of the original chapel, which they demolished in 1833, to expose the front of the third chapel. This chapel was rebuilt in 1881 and a new front, ceiling, and organ bay were added in 1922. It closed about ten years ago but is retained as a Christian centre.

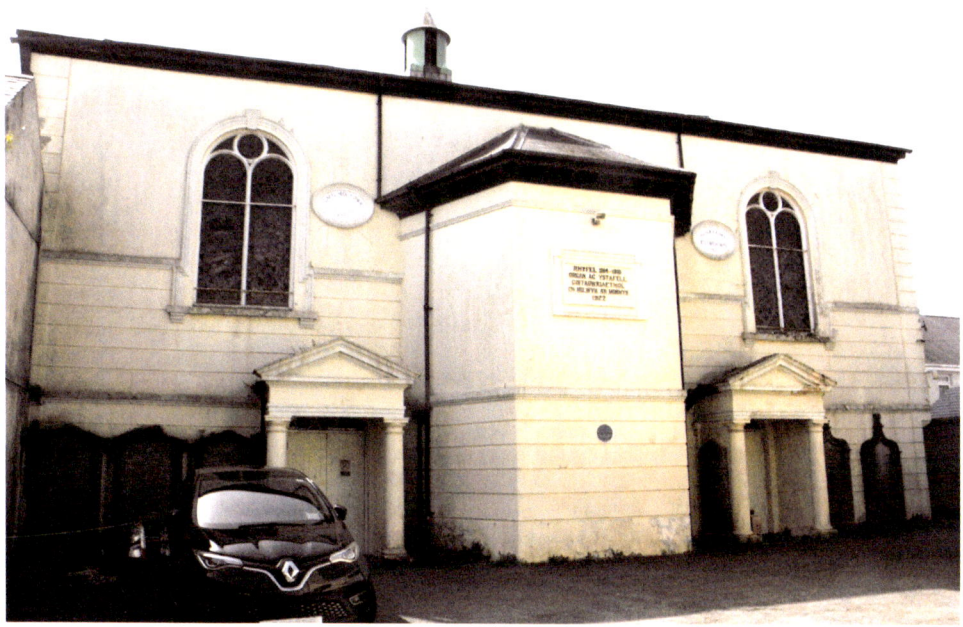

Welsh Calvinistic Methodist Chapel.

The frontage of the chapel is bounded by a long wall and a pair of pedimented porches on Tuscan columns each supporting a large arched window. An unusual feature of the chapel is the wine-glass-shaped pulpit with its curved flight of steps. A similar pulpit exists in the Baptist Chapel, Lammas Street (Capel Heol Awst), but these are rare and usually removed during renovations. The chapel also has several noteworthy monuments. Later three churches were set up in Carmarthen as branches of Water Street Chapel, namely Babell, Pensarn (1849), Zion, Carmarthen (1850), and Bethania, Carmarthen (1902). Zion is now a camera shop and the local Muslim community own Bethania.

Initially considered as a replacement cathedral for the dioceses of St David, the church served the town's main Welsh-speaking Anglican congregation. In the early part of the nineteenth century, a local benefactor donated land in Lammas Street for the construction of St Paul's Anglican Church. However, when they discovered they had not been invited to the ceremonial laying of the foundation stone on 27 November 1824, they withdrew the gift of land. A new site for the church was found in Picton Terrace, and in 1837 the Anglican Church of St David (Eglwys Dewi Sant) opened its doors.

In charge was Revd David Archard Williams, former student and headteacher of the Carmarthen Boys Grammar School. Williams had also been chaplain to the town's workhouse and asylum, editor of the *Carmarthen Journal*, director of the gasworks, and a county magistrate. He was responsible for the siting and establishment of the Training College in Carmarthen (now known as Trinity St David University) and for building the Model School in St Catherine Street.

The church was initially built for Welsh speakers to worship in their own language, but when English-speaking worshippers began taking over the affairs of the church, they

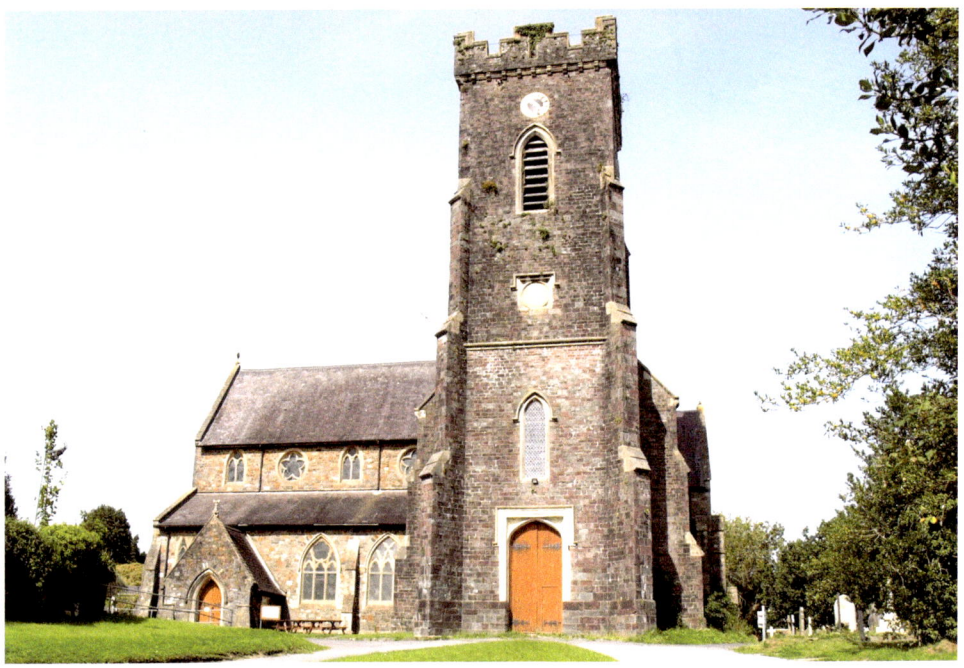

Anglican Church of Saint David.

lobbied for the Welsh language to be restored in the church and for the English speakers to construct their own place of worship.

Eventually another parish church, Christ Church, was built in 1867 to cater to the English congregation of this expanding parish, allowing St David's to concentrate on providing Welsh services for Welsh-speaking parishioners (see Christ Church below).

Between 1912 and 1913 the church underwent a major restoration, followed by further alterations during 1938. It was designated a Grade II listed building on 19 May 1981. Storm damage in November 2003 resulted in the church's closure. After decades of neglect the church and graveyard were dilapidated and in 2011 it was sold for £1. Shortly afterwards the Church in Wales took responsibility for the upkeep and the Thomas and Elizabeth Mayhook Charity was formed in 2015 to preserve, upkeep and maintain the cemetery.

Revd Williams and member Colonel Scott were instrumental in the construction of an English-speaking Anglican Church. Scott had arrived in Carmarthen to create a police force during the Rebecca Riots in 1843. After which he stayed in the town and became Carmarthenshire's first Chief Constable. On 2 September 1867, during the National Eisteddfod at Carmarthen, they laid the foundation stone for Christ Church (Eglwys Crist), in Lammas Street, upon the original site of St David's Church.

The colossal size of the church reflects its need to accommodate the soldiers garrisoned in the town. It was consecrated on 21 September 1869 and the organ was added in 1873, with the organ chamber and vestry following in 1900. The choir stalls and rails were removed to St David's Church during the 1930s.'

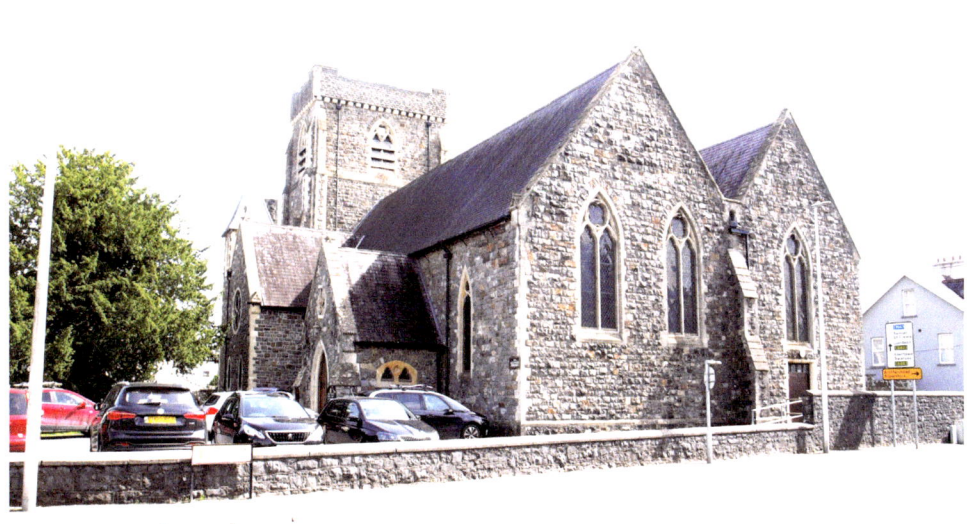

Christ Church.

The original tower had a steep pyramid-shaped slate roof, which was replaced by battlements in 1965. Mystery surrounds the tower's first bell, which was found on the quay at Swansea in 1864. The bell had been used as ballast and was inscribed 'from a church in Santiago, Chile'. It's believed that this bell may have come from the Church of the Society of Jesus, which caught fire on 8 December 1863, killing between 2,000 and 3,000 worshipers. The Santiago church originally housed five extremely heavy metal bells, with inscriptions in Latin and Spanish. According to records, four were sold for scrap to a smelting business in Swansea.

The bells were not scrapped but saved. Three were presented to All Saints Church in Oystermouth and one to St Thomas's, Neath. These four have since returned to Chile, but the fifth was never recovered. Was it bought by the Swansea smelting business, but not shipped or manifested with the other four? It is highly improbable that such a large and serviceable bell would have been removed from a church in Chile whilst in use. Because of their expense and religious association bells are usually reused when a church is rebuilt or replaced. A decision was made not to rebuild the Church of the Society of Jesus and to sell its five bells for scrap. Could it be that Christ Church is home to the missing fifth bell?

4. Turbulent Times

In 1285 King Edward I rationalised law and order in Carmarthen, introducing what he called 'Watch and Ward'. This system preserved peace through the appointment of community members who conducted patrols and undertook sentry duties, during which they watched for fires and protected property and citizens from criminals. The night shift was known as the Watch and the day shift the Ward. Itinerant traders had to produce sureties that showed their identity and business interests and the town's gates remained closed from dusk to dawn with its streets under curfew. Sixteen men kept the watch in the cities, twelve in boroughs, and four in smaller communities.

In Carmarthen, by the turn of the nineteenth century that task fell to just one man, who became known as Wil y Lon. Wil stood for a medieval system of law enforcement that during its 500 years had failed to keep step with social changes and advances in science and technology. These developments created opportunities for social advancement, economic gain and commercial expansion for some, and hardship, poverty and disadvantage for others. It was a system incapable of responding to the storm of social unrest and injustice that had been gathering over centuries, and whose clouds were about to burst over Carmarthen.

Despite the best efforts of the town's dignitaries, politicians and men of vision, Carmarthen could not pull free from its medieval legacy. The people of Carmarthen had gained a national notoriety for their drunkenness, brutal brawling and importuning of visitors and merchants.

The town bristled with tricksters and gamesters. Near Dark Gate sizeable crowds jostled to watch bulls being baited, and on one occasion saw the landlord of the Boar's Head, who ventured too close, gored to death by a terrified bull. Cockfighting and badger baiting were also commonplace. Pickpockets prevailed and prostitutes openly plied their trade, and immorality and the very worst of men lurked hand in hand in the many ale and gin houses. Carmarthen had gained a reputation for being a feisty, violent, unsettled and loathsome place, with all the character and charisma of a Wild West town.

When the 'Carmarthen Mob' bonded, as they often did in the 1700s, the outcome was frequently a bloody and ferocious demonstration of their discontent. Occasionally their rowdy behaviour was all their own doing, such as their demonstration against the local Jacobites in 1745, which reportedly left the town filled with 'fire and smoke'. The 1757 food shortages saw the 'Mob' of over 100 men riot through the streets for several days. During the cheese riot of 1818 the 'Mob' ransacked a ship and twice prevented the export of a much-needed shipment of cheese.

On other occasions, persons of note and influence would use the 'Mob' for their own ends. There was a long-running tradition in Carmarthen of violence occurring

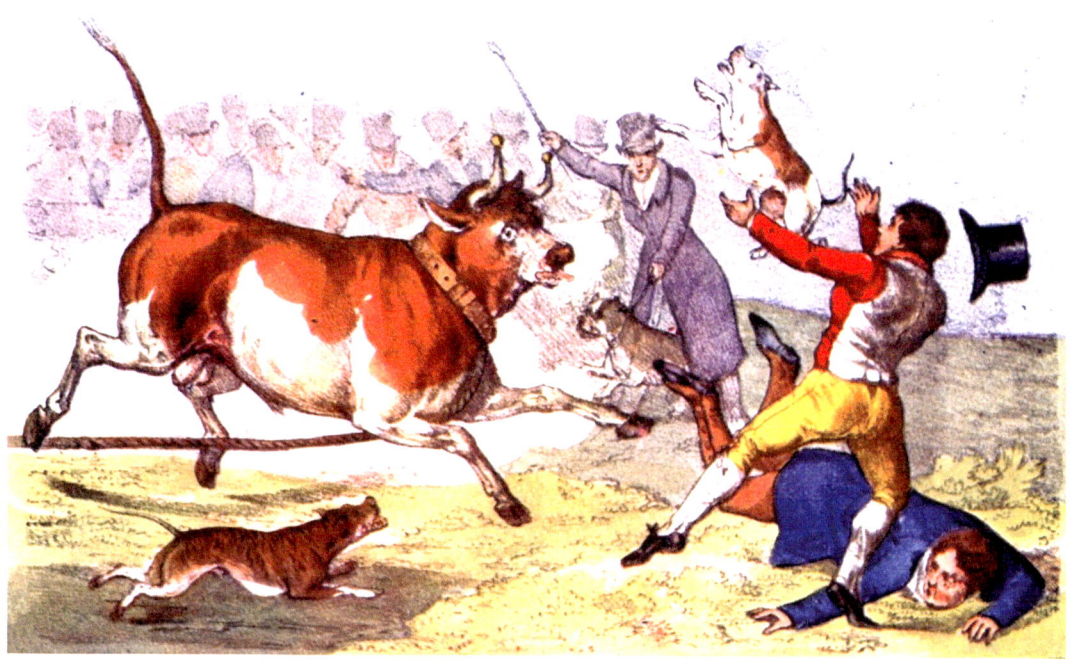

Eighteenth-century illustration of bull-baiting. (PD)

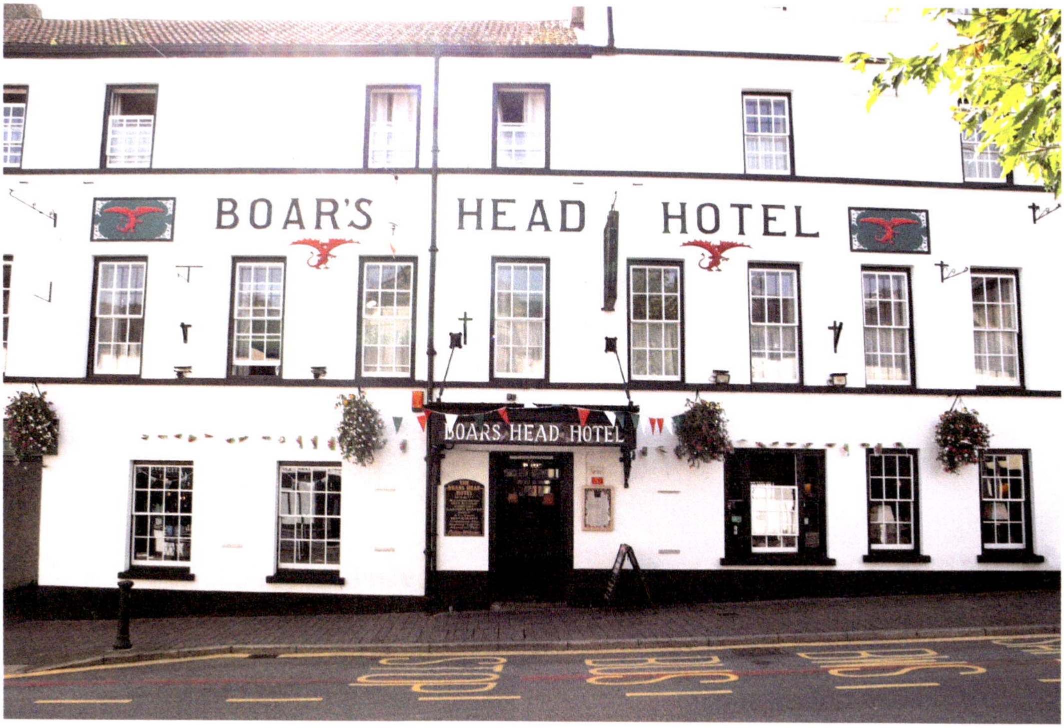

The Boar's Head.

during parliamentary and borough elections, which all too often turned the Guildhall and surrounding areas into a battleground between the 'Mob' and the party they opposed.

In 1796 London banker Dorrien Magens was illegally elected at the borough elections. The Carmarthen Mob protested and fought a running battle through the town. Pistols were fired and a supporter of Magens injured. The 'Mob' continued its rampage trying to demolish the opposition's property and setting fire to any house they found barricaded.

Successive elections were fiercely contested and policed by a handful of newly sworn special constables and ineffective regulars. At the first sign of trouble both surrendered and defaulted their duties to the local militia, who in their eagerness to join the melee regularly deployed without the mayor's authority. The outcome was always the same: the staves of the 'Mob' and the bayonets of the militia left a bloody wake of destruction, beatings, and broken bones.

There was no town in Wales so troubled, so distressed, and so destitute of law and order in those times as Carmarthen. The levels of corruption, violence and public disorder were so overwhelming that the town's beleaguered magistrates felt powerless and unable to cope with the level of routine criminality.

A seemingly desperate situation deteriorated further during the Reform Elections of 1831 when the former 'Blue' Tory party member and ten-year MP for Carmarthen, John Jones, a vehement opponent of reform, swapped parties to become a 'Red'. His opposition was the 'Blue' veteran of the Battle of the Nile, Captain John Phillips RN. The Carmarthen Mob pledged its fidelity to the 'Blue' Tory party and John Phillips.

No party could be certain of its hold on the borough, but the town's corporation had been dominated by the 'Blues' since the last charter was granted in 1764. It wasn't long before the traditional election violence began. The battle started inside the Guildhall on Friday 29 April, where several constables and administrators were badly assaulted before being swallowed by the rowdy mob. When the preliminary addresses were concluded an unpleasant Tory mob stormed the hall, causing Jones, his allies, and election staff to fear for their lives.

The violence spilled into the surrounding streets. Further murderous threats were made against Jones. Lacking police to contain the rioters, the mayor could not read out the Riot Act and the election was abandoned. The tumultuous 'Blue Mob', brandishing many weapons, began assaulting anybody suspected of being a 'Red.'

The following day was a repeat of the previous when the 'Blue Mob' rioted, meted out further savagery and threatened to kill Jones and any 'Reds' present. Chief Constable James Evans, his officers and specials, including the sheriff, had either taken flight or hidden. For a second time, the election could not continue.

On Monday 2 May the Guildhall was once more opened to complete voting. On this occasion there was no sign of John Jones or his supporters, no special or regular constables were in attendance, and the town's sheriffs and mayor were nowhere to be found. In Jones's absence the Tories claimed a victory for Phillips and paraded him around the town in a boat.

Outraged at the town's failure to lawfully complete the election, Parliament sent the 93rd Regiment (Argyll and Sutherland Highlanders) then stationed at Brecon to retake the town. The 93rd arrived after two days of lawlessness with bayonets fixed. They soon quelled the rioting and within hours had secured seventeen ringleaders of the Carmarthen Mob in the borough gaol.

With order restored, the troops returned to Brecon. Days later on 28 May, the seventeen members of the 'Mob' were released from gaol on bail. A large crowd of coracle men, boatmen, fishermen and men of the Carmarthen Mob greeted them triumphantly. They were paraded through the town to the sound of chanting, singing, breaking glass and repeated gunfire. More rioting ensued, and magistrates appealed to the Home Secretary for help.

Their pleas fell on deaf ears. A blunt response said the responsibility of policing the town was theirs and theirs alone. The political violence added to the existing disorder among the long-suffering, starving and mainly illiterate citizens. With the unfettered 'Blue Mob' regaining control of the town, the situation took a turn for the worse.

Several serious fights broke out along the quay between disparate factions of coracle and fishermen from Llanstephan and Ferryside, determined to settle long-standing grudges. Firearms were routinely discharged. Further appeals to the Home Secretary for help were disregarded and as the disorder continued magistrates were forced to recruit special constables from the ranks of the Carmarthen Mob itself.

The chief constable equipped twenty-four specials with wooden staves. These men, unsurprisingly, weren't enough to prevent peace from being breached, and when faced with a riot ran away. Of the twenty-four staves issued, only six were returned. The rest entered service with the 'Mob.'

Authority totally collapsed on 10 June, when magistrates told the Home Secretary, they had no means of preventing riot or violence, that they had done their duty diligently but could no longer be held accountable for the future peace of the town or any loss of life.

The 'Blue' seventeen appeared at the Assizes on 29 July to face charges. The jury consisted of 'Red' burgesses, led by a 'Red' magistrate, who unsurprisingly found enough evidence for the seventeen to be tried at the petty court and duly committed the men to trial. The petty court's jury was also drawn from 'Red' jurors. The seventeen's counsel defended them admirably, arguing the injustice of their situation and pleading for the case to be heard by a jury from outside the borough. This was agreed, and that jury delivered a unanimous verdict of 'not guilty.'

Another triumph for the Carmarthen 'Blues' led to more civil disorder after their victorious procession through the town. Enough was enough. The town could no longer go unrepresented, and the House of Commons issued a new election writ for 20 August. Yet again, magistrates faced the prospect of a bloody and fierce election and once more, they appealed to the Home Secretary for military aid to deal with the expected disturbances.

Keen not to use the military as a deterrent, infantry of the 98th Prince of Wales's Foot Regiment and a troop from the 14th Dragoon Guards were sent to Llandeilo. Six officers of the newly formed Metropolitan Police were sent to Carmarthen to support the discredited chief constable and his four delinquent constables. Men from Llanelli and Pembrey collieries made up the larger part of the special constables sworn in for the event.

Police reinforcements and the proximity of the military gave optimism to all concerned that their deployment would be unnecessary. On the evening of the election, Mayor Daniel Prytherch showed the six uniformed Metropolitan officers and a party of special constables around the town. The sound of shots being fired, smashing glass, and shouting in Spilman Street was the signal that rioting had begun.

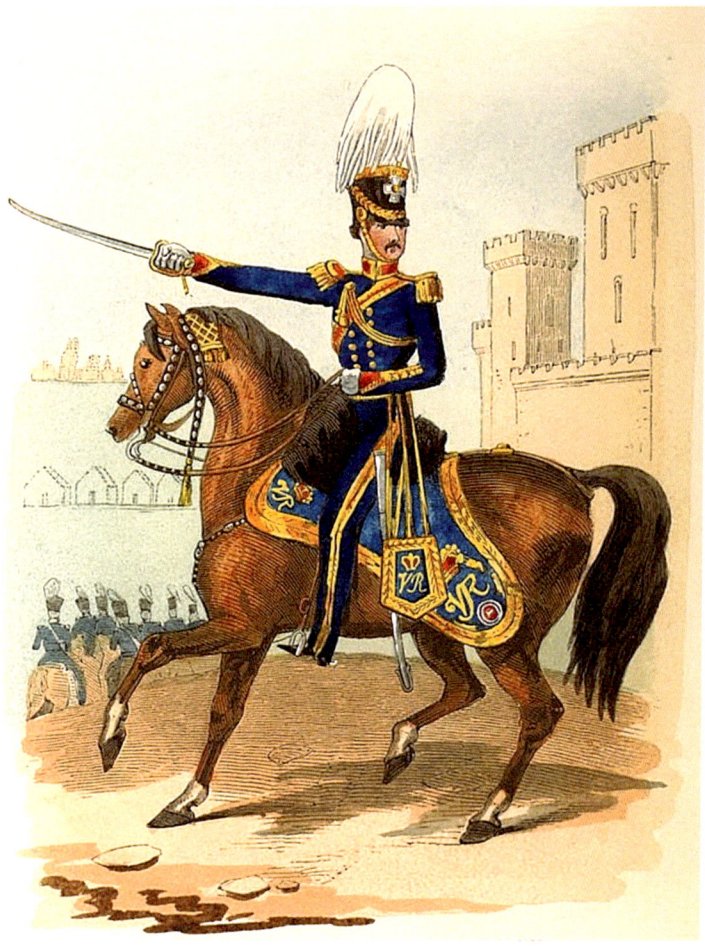

14th Dragoon Guards. (PD)

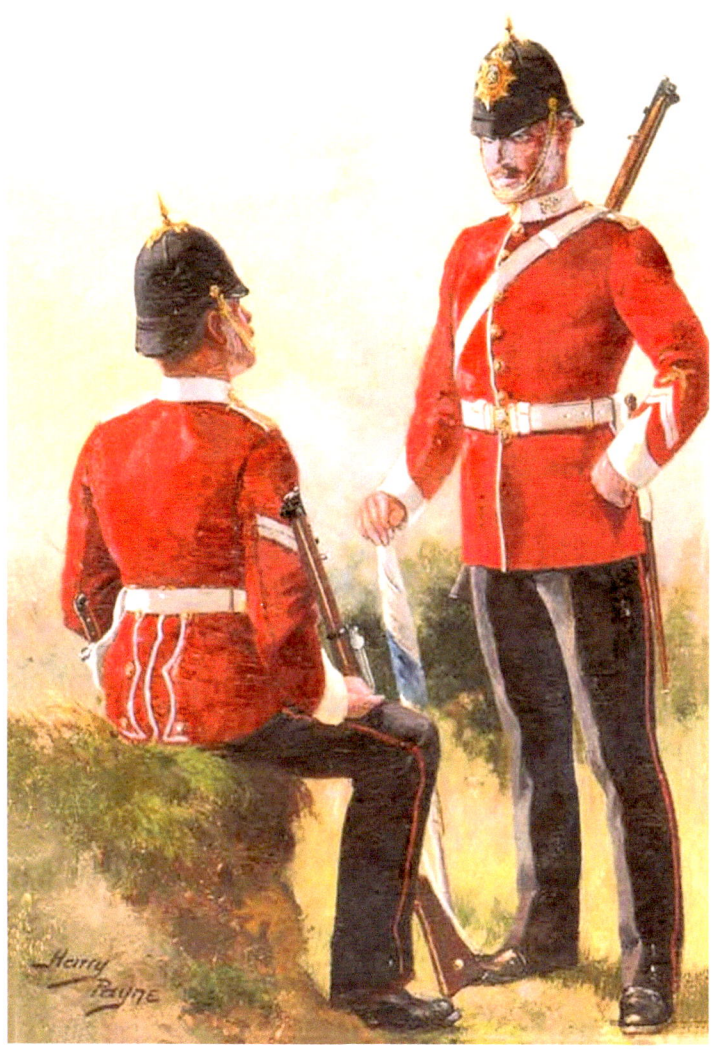

98th Prince of Wales's
Foot Regiment. (HP)

The small band of law enforcers tried to put down the riot and entered Spilman Street. There was a fight, and one constable was struck on the head with a club, while others were assaulted with rocks. Numerous offenders were arrested, and several constables injured, one seriously, being rendered unfit for duty for two days. Throughout the night large bodies of men prowled the streets, bent on causing mischief. Several clashes took place between the 'Mob' and the police, who had become the focus of their hatred and violence.

The following day, amidst a highly charged electorate, the election of a Member of Parliament for the Borough of Carmarthen continued. When events became heated, the election was adjourned until the following Monday. The election took three and a half days to complete, each day more unruly than the day before.

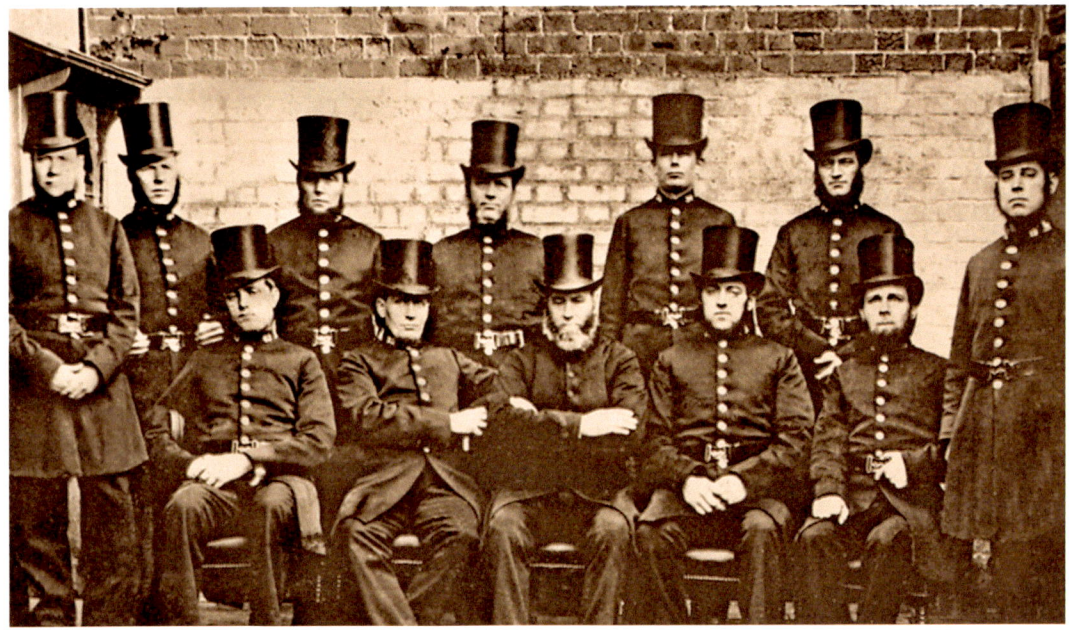

Metropolitan Police, *c.* 1830. (PD)

On the Monday when a show of hands was sought for the 'Blue' Phillips, a cacophony of jeering began. So tempestuous was their reaction that several were ejected. When they were arrested supporters attacked the arresting officers. So great was the ferocity the police threatened to use firearms. That night gangs took to the streets, threatening the lives and property of the opposition. The mayor, expecting the army to help, mobilised the local militia to cover until they arrived.

Tuesday saw no violence until the evening when the 'Mob' once more roamed the streets smashing windows. Magistrate David Jones, a young 'Red,' and several special constables were brutally assaulted during 'Mob' attacks. Wednesday was noisy but passed without serious incident.

On Thursday, a result was finally achieved. John Jones emerged victorious from the Guildhall only to be stoned. The packed square erupted into violence, arrests were made, several constables and the chief constable were wounded, beaten so badly that murders would have been committed had help not arrived. The fighting became a battle that spilled into Dark Gate and continued for hours. Both the militia and regular troops were put on alert as sporadic rioting continued for several days, but eventually the police cleared the streets without intervention by either the militia or regular forces.

Four days after the election, the town finally reverted to normal levels of crime and disorder to the point the magistrates felt it was secure. A request was made to the Home Secretary for two of the Metropolitan officers to remain until after the Charter Day elections on 3 October. These were held to select a new mayor, two sheriffs, six magistrates and a treasurer and were always contentious, giving another opportunity for

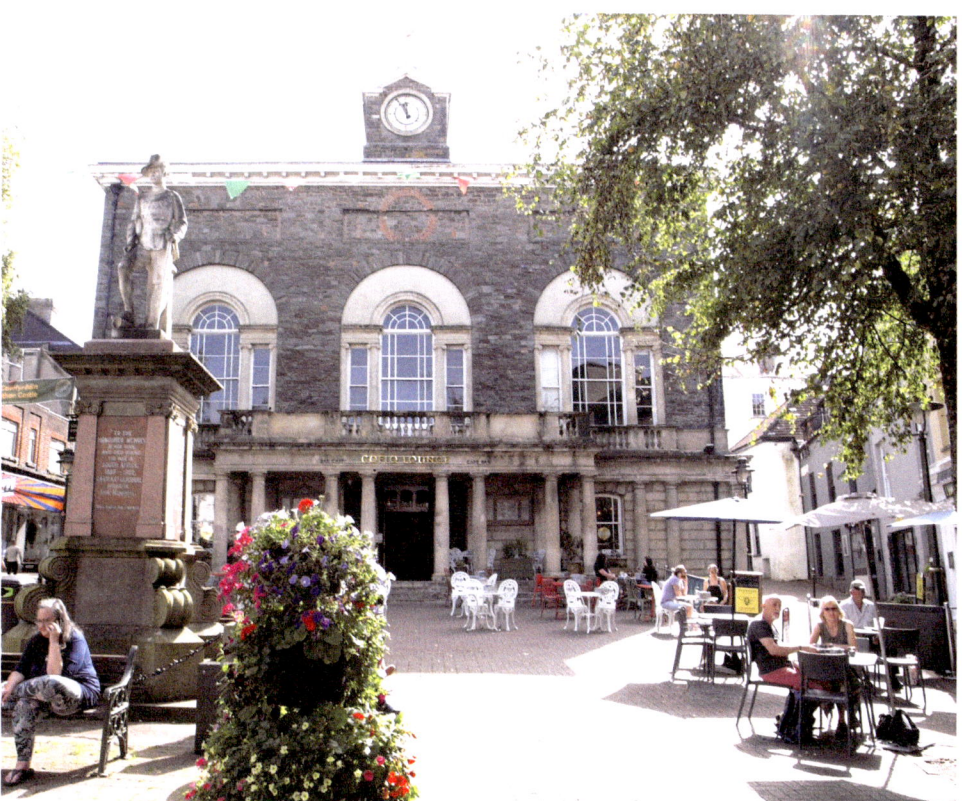

The Guildhall.

the town's 'Red' and 'Blue' factions to riot in the absence of adequate law enforcement provisions.

The Charter Day elections did not disappoint the Carmarthen Mob, and those looking to settle old and recent scores. What can only be described as 'a Battle Royal' took place. The election held in the Guildhall had been heated but concluded with the re-election of Daniel Prytherch as mayor and seemed to have passed without incident. Then, as the polls closed, an attack was launched against the constables stationed in the hall. Their assailants robbed them of their staves and used them to batter the constables before forcing them into the street. There attacks continued and the severely injured constables sought safety among the neighbouring houses.

The militia formed a guard outside the hall, holding the mob at bay with bayonets fixed and muskets loaded. The election of other officials was adjourned to the following day so adequate measures could be taken. Police looked for and locked up ringleaders of the Guildhall affray and then fought a grim night-time battle through the town in pursuit of stick-carrying gangs intent on breaking windows and damaging property. Magistrates used every means at their disposal to persuade as many men as possible to become special constables.

In the morning, the militia resumed their position outside the Guildhall, while the police, the walking wounded, and newly sworn specials, were more strategically deployed. The result was an uneventful election. In time the town returned to a state of normality in which the odd protest by the 'Mob' against market tolls was adequately managed by the five regular officers and two secondees from London. Carmarthen 'short arm' of the law had prevailed.

If 1831 had taught the Corporation anything about law and order it was the need for an effective police force capable of keeping the peace, one that the 'Mob' would fear and respect. So it was that the foundations for a police force were laid when John Lazenby, one of the London constables whose leadership had stood out during the riots, was made chief of four regular constables, among them former Chief Constable James Evans.

Both men would face the wrath of the 'Mob' again during the 1832 Charter Day elections, a violent affair involving riot, gunfire and military action. An incident that occurred at the Star and Garter, Spilman Street, is of special note. The 'Blue Mob,' looking for trouble, was shocked by the landlord firing shots into their crowd, wounding some offenders. They retaliated with fury, but the landlord continued to load and fire his pistols into the fierce rabble. The mob smashed his windows, pulled the frames out, attacked the stonework and pulled the building down around him.

The police, unable to reach the besieged landlord, waited for the military who arrived with bayonets fixed. They cleared a path that allowed the mayor to read the Riot Act

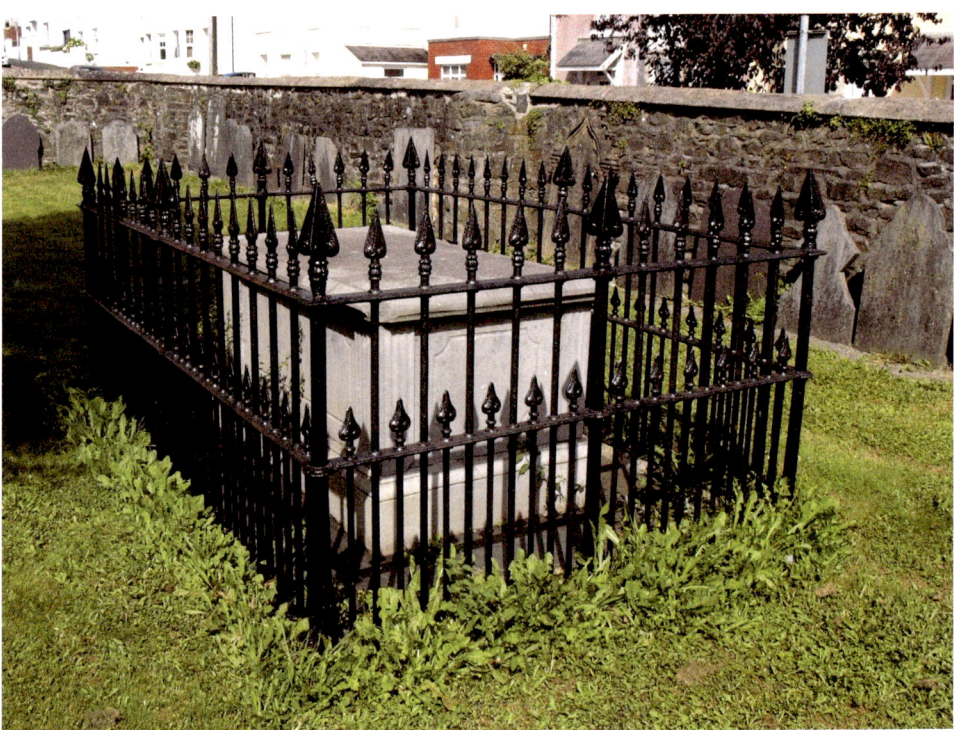

Tomb of Mayor Daniel Prytherch, St David's.

and the police to reach the landlord. Arrests were made and peace once more returned to the town.

After the Carmarthen Charter Day riots a select committee conducted an inquiry into the state of Municipal Corporations across England and Wales focussing firmly on Carmarthen. Their report, produced in 1834, made grim reading. They found that both red and blue parties were equally guilty of using political influences to control judges, rig juries, appoint magistrates and burgesses, and bias the outcome of judgements to further their own interests.

They condemned the Corporation for flouting King George III's charter by keeping key decision making in the hands of a few burgesses who favoured their own supporters. They also condemned the Corporation for electoral fraud, wholesale forgery of qualifications by those seeking election and, in addition, found massive debts which virtually bankrupted the borough. In addition, they found land had been fraudulently disposed of, and fiscal misconduct had been taking place for over forty years.

They found the gaoler was a burgess of the incumbent political party and, as such, in their service, as were his predecessors. The chief constable of the police had no effective control over his twelve constables who they described as 'very ineffective'. They also found the system of hiring and firing constables was tainted by the biases of voting for or against the incumbent Corporation.

To Carmarthen's eternal shame it led the kingdom in political graft, corruption and mismanagement that included acts of betrayal, deception, bribery and nepotism to the reduction of public interests. Carmarthen made political history by being the cause for the creation of the Municipal Corporations Act of 1835. The act swept away the public laws of the ancient royal charter, replacing them with new laws that addressed the grievous wrongs in the governance of municipal corporations. Carmarthen was seen as the most politically corrupt borough in Britain.

It would take several decades before Carmarthen's police established themselves as a force to be reckoned with and capable of asserting authority on the most turbulent town in Wales. That period would prove to be a painful growing and learning experience during which the spectre of lawlessness hovered over them like thunder, and like a bad penny would from time to time turn up when least expected.

5. Merlin, Druids and Bards

The earliest mention of Merlin's association with the town dates to when the legions of the Roman Empire having arrived in Carmarthen took oversight of Caer Myrddin, the pagan city of the Demetae tribe. They discovered a shrine dedicated to Myrddin (Merlin) the Celtic god of poetry and prophecy, being worshipped by the Demetae and local druids, a learned class of Celtic priests, teachers and judges.

After the Romans left, 600 years passed before the Normans reached Carmarthen in 1093. They discovered a monastic order ruling a dilapidated post-Roman settlement. At the heart of the community lay a pagan church, Llan Teulydawc, where they worshipped the Welsh Celtic St Teulyddog. When the Normans built St John's Priory on the site of 'Llan Teulydawc,' they dedicated it to the Christian St John the Evangelist and Teulyddog. It was here at the priory that the earliest surviving complete manuscript written in the Welsh language was penned.

Known as the Black Book of Carmarthen because of the colour of its binding, the book has the Mabinogion, eleven mystical tales of Welsh Celtic folklore, tradition and history, previously passed by word of mouth through generations by early Welsh bards. The first four are prose that gives us accounts of the royal families of Wales and themes of friendship, war, revenge, redemption, oppression, enchantment, loyalty, love, fidelity, magic, and grotesque beasts. The other seven include Arthurian legends, tales of fairy heroes, Celtic warriors, along with the quests and adventures of Arthur's knights.

The book includes stories about the Holy Grail, and the great wizard and alchemist Merlin, described as a prophet, wild man of the woods, and a powerful magician who prophesied the coming of King Arthur and the defeat of the Anglo-Saxons.

Today Merlin is synonymous with Carmarthen (Caerfyrddin), which translates as the 'fortress of Merlin' and is locally known as Merlin's Town. One of the legends of Merlin associated with the town is the 'Old Oak,' the 'Carmarthen Oak' or, as it is best known, 'Merlin's Oak'.

This tree is thought to have been planted in 1660 to celebrate the return to the throne of Charles II. Merlin's Oak formerly stood in the centre of the town on the junction between Priory Street and Oak Lane. By the nineteenth century legends had developed connecting the tree to Merlin, and during the mid-nineteenth century it had become a gathering point for local drinkers, revellers and wayward children.

This situation became too much for one local trader who in 1856 poisoned the tree in protest of their 'incessant and unruly behaviour'. When the tree eventually died the town held its breath in fear of the fulfilment of a long-held prophecy associated with the tree. 'When Myrddin's tree shall tumble down, then shall fall Carmarthen Town.'

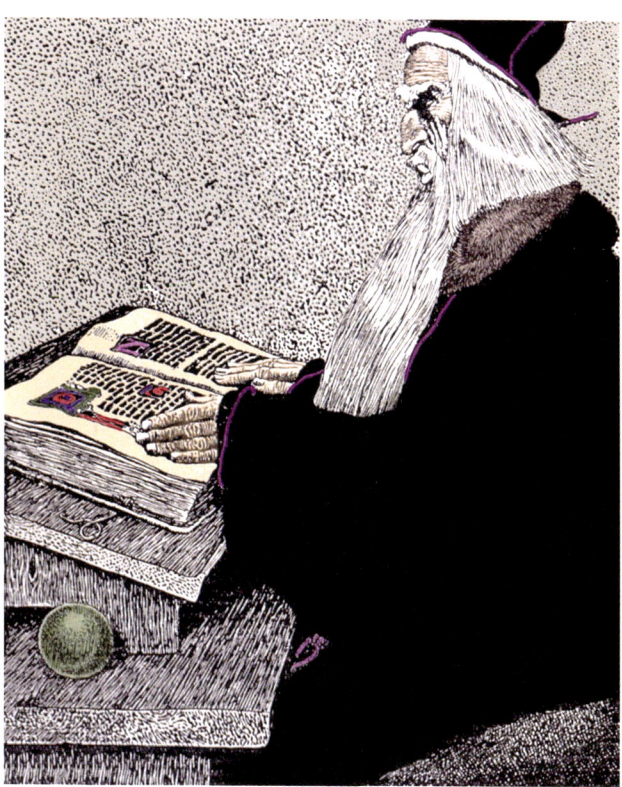

Merlin. (HP)

As the dead tree decayed the town kept bracing it to prevent the prophecy from coming true. Cement was even poured around the base and bands of steel placed around its trunk to hold it in place. When rotten fragments of the gnarled old tree were eventually removed in 1978, the town didn't fall but it suffered its worst floods in living memory. A branch can be viewed in the Carmarthen Museum in a small display case. Fragments of the tree are also preserved in the foyer of St Peter's Civic Hall, Nott Square. While along King Street the JD Wetherspoon pub is named Yr Hen Dderwen after the old oak tree.

Legend also has it that the cave where Merlin was born, and which served as his home, is hidden in the nearby tree-covered hill Bryn Myrddin (Merlin's Hill), on the A40. According to folklore when the sorceress Vivien gained Merlin's trust through enchantment, he taught her many spells, which she used to imprison him in the cave. Time passed and the cave's exact location became lost, leaving Merlin locked in the bonds of Vivien's enchantment. On still nights some claim they can hear the clanking of Merlin's chains coming from the hill.

Also on Merlin's Hill is a large standing Neolithic stone where the mighty magician supposedly hid his treasure. Tradition has it that Merlin predicted that one day a raven would drink a man's blood from it. Coincidence or curse? In 1860 a man hunting for the treasure was digging around the base of the stone when the earth gave way, causing it

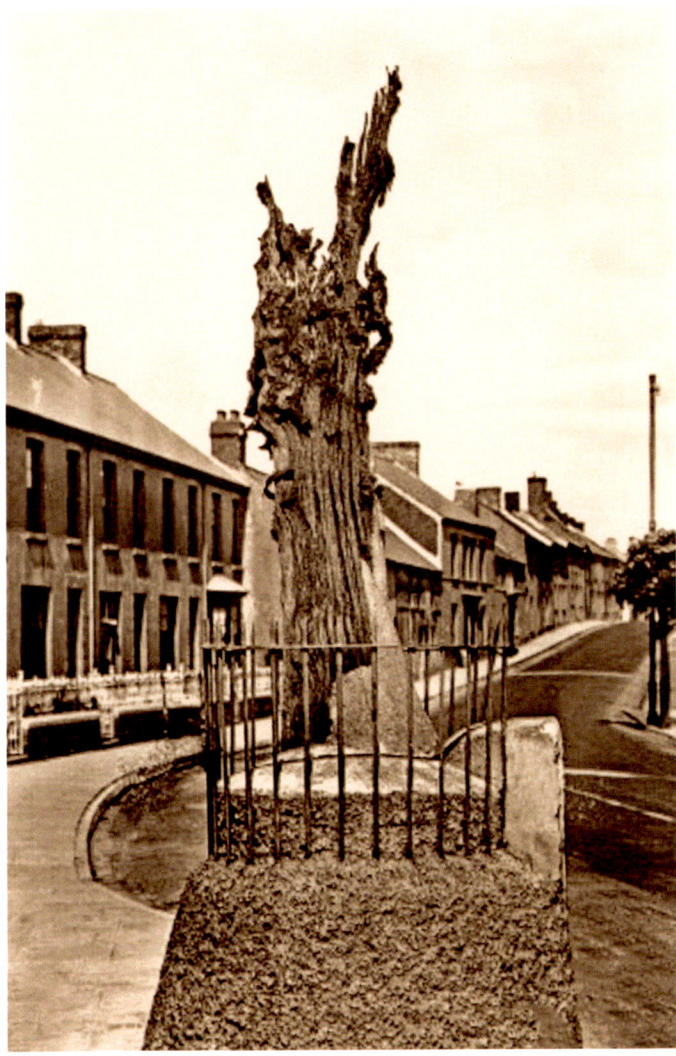

The Old Oak. (PD)

to fall and crush him to death. The landowner ordered the stone to be placed back in its original position, which it was, though it took five horses to move it.

Within the town are many references to Merlin, and within Merlin's Walk, in Blue Street, the magician's association with the town is commemorated by a wonderful wooden statue of him.

Until writing became widespread the only means of keeping the deeds and feats of notable people, places and events in history alive was through the storytelling, poetry and music of druids and bards. As time passed druids and bards disappeared, and in Wales there was a real risk that the Welsh language, stories, customs and culture might die out. Eisteddfods (Eisteddfodau), competitive festivals of music and poetry, were created to prevent this. The earliest is believed to have taken place during the sixth century.

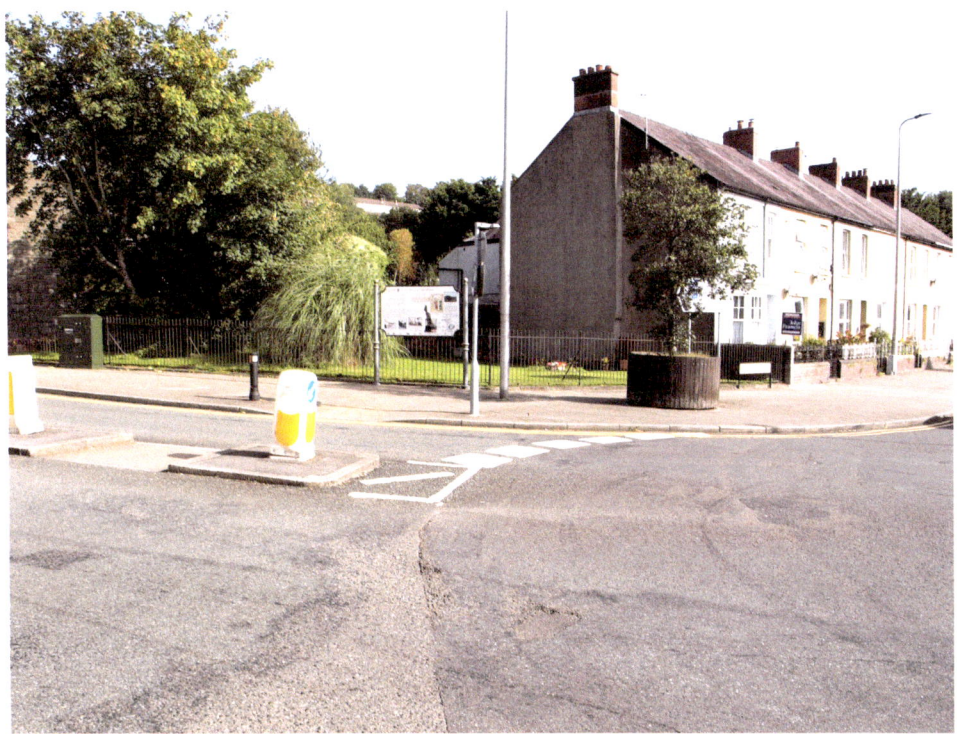

Oak Lane today.

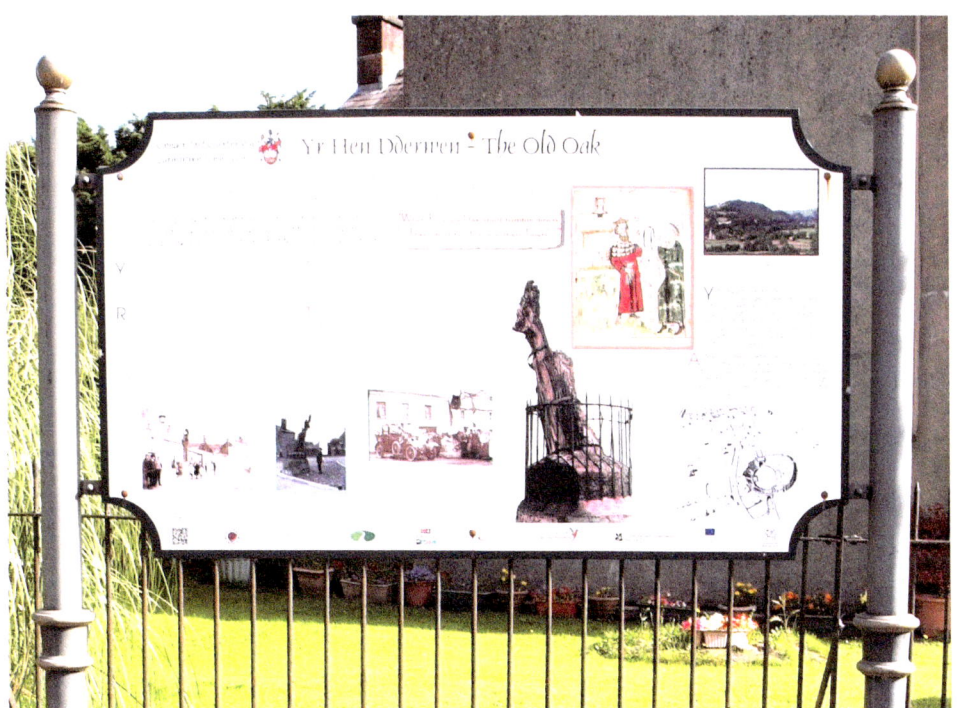

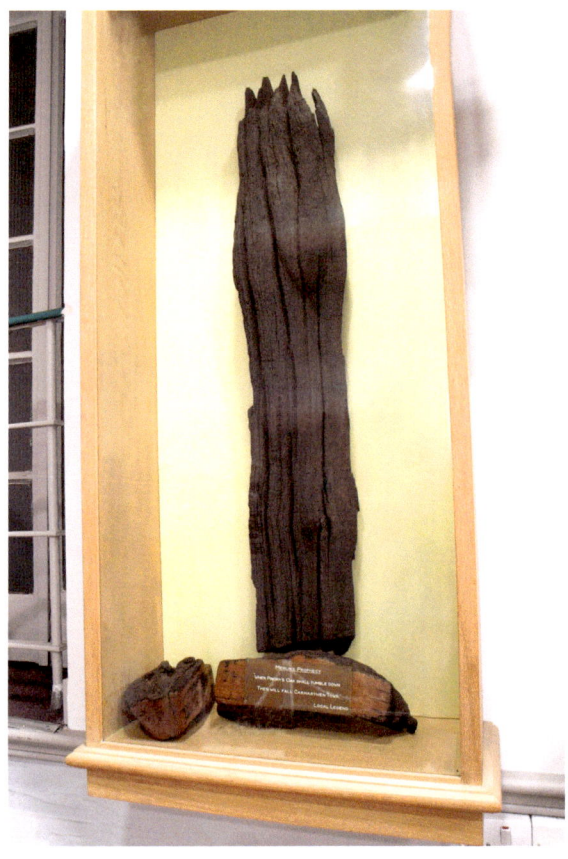

St Peter's Civic Hall.

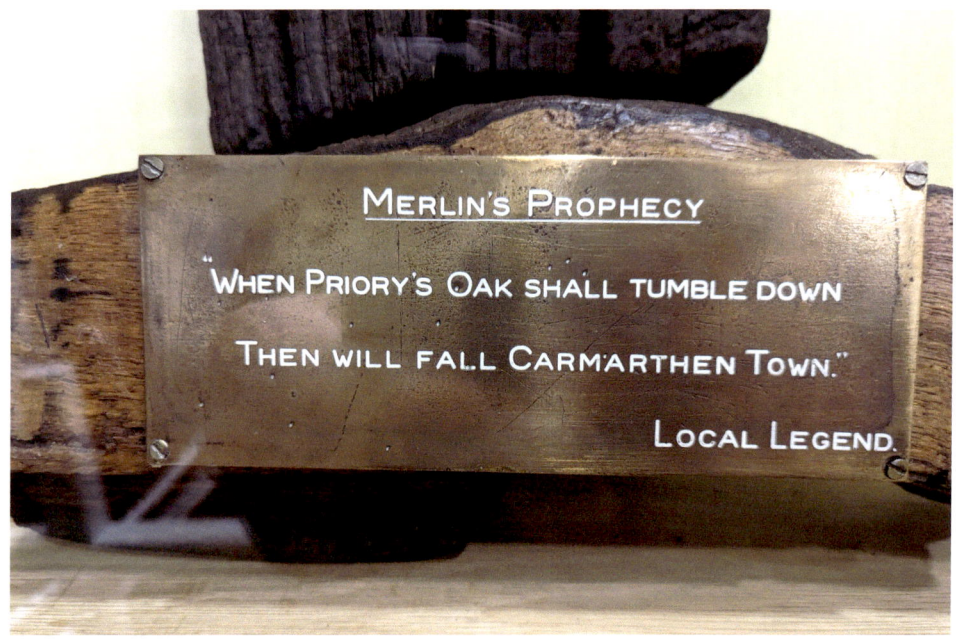

MERLIN'S PROPHECY

"WHEN PRIORY'S OAK SHALL TUMBLE DOWN

THEN WILL FALL CARMARTHEN TOWN."

LOCAL LEGEND.

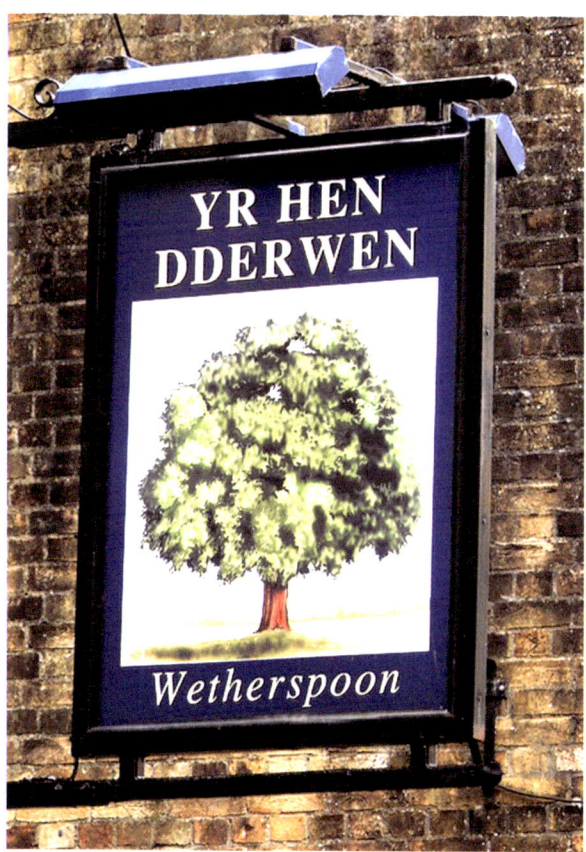

Wetherspoons pub sign.

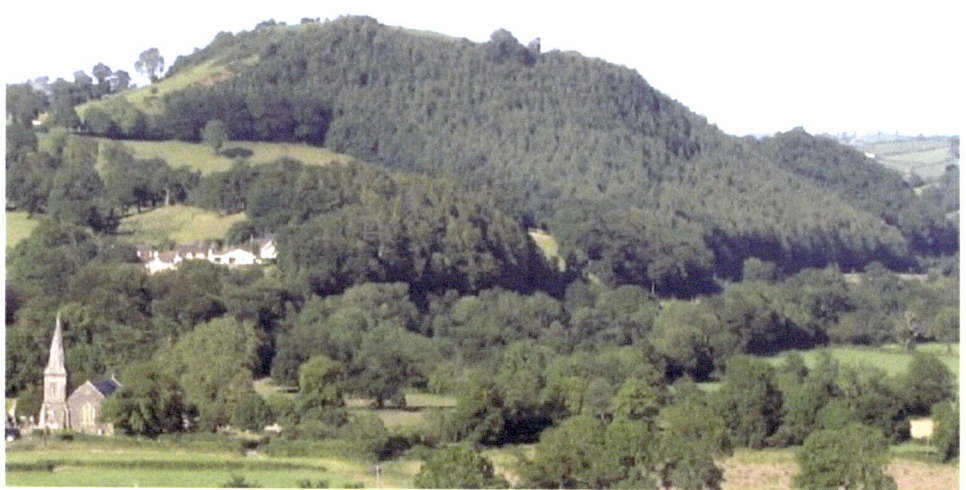

Bryn Myrddin. (ND)

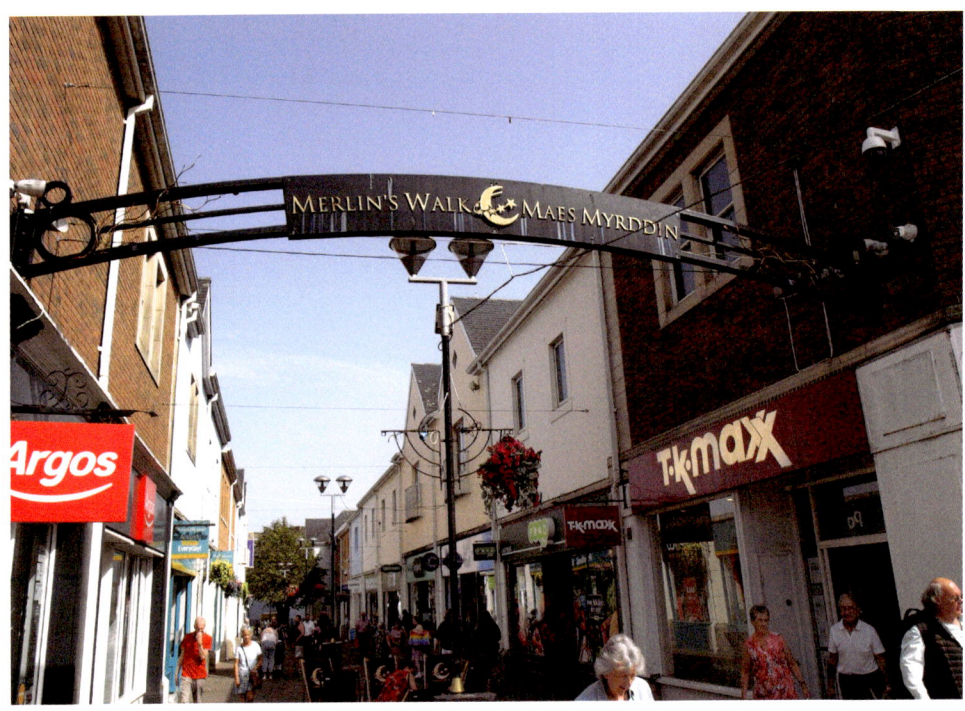

Merlin's Walk.

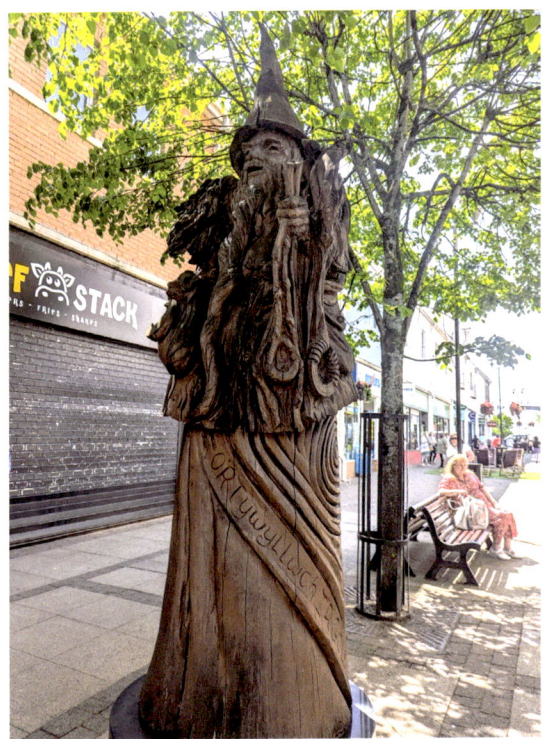

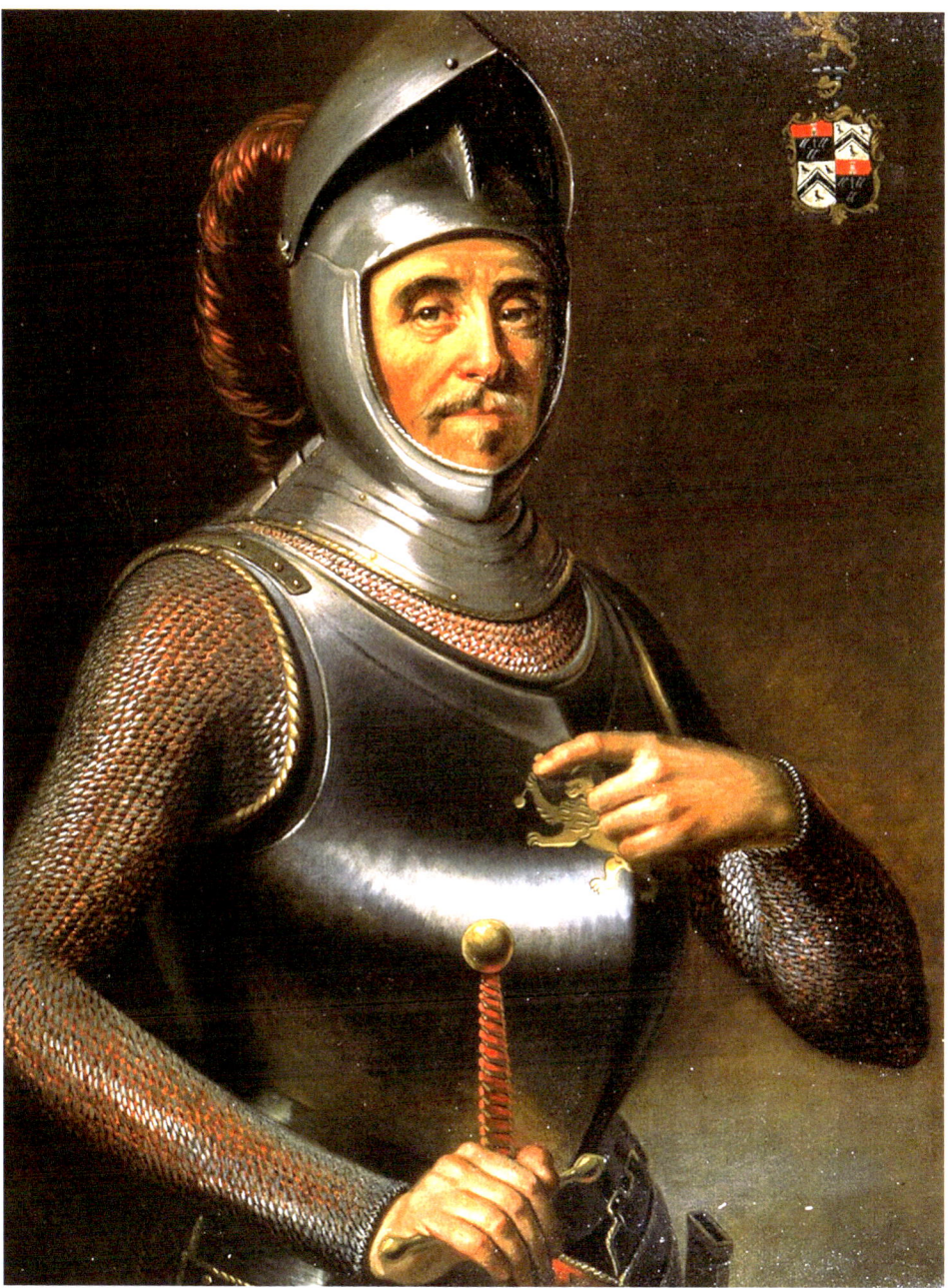

Rhys ap Gruffydd. (JPVD)

A prominent patron of the Welsh bards, Lord Rhys ap Gruffydd hosted the forerunner of the modern National Eisteddfod at Cardigan Castle in 1176. The eisteddfod involved bards and minstrels from all over Wales. The winners of the poetry and music competitions received the prestigious award of an ornately carved chair.

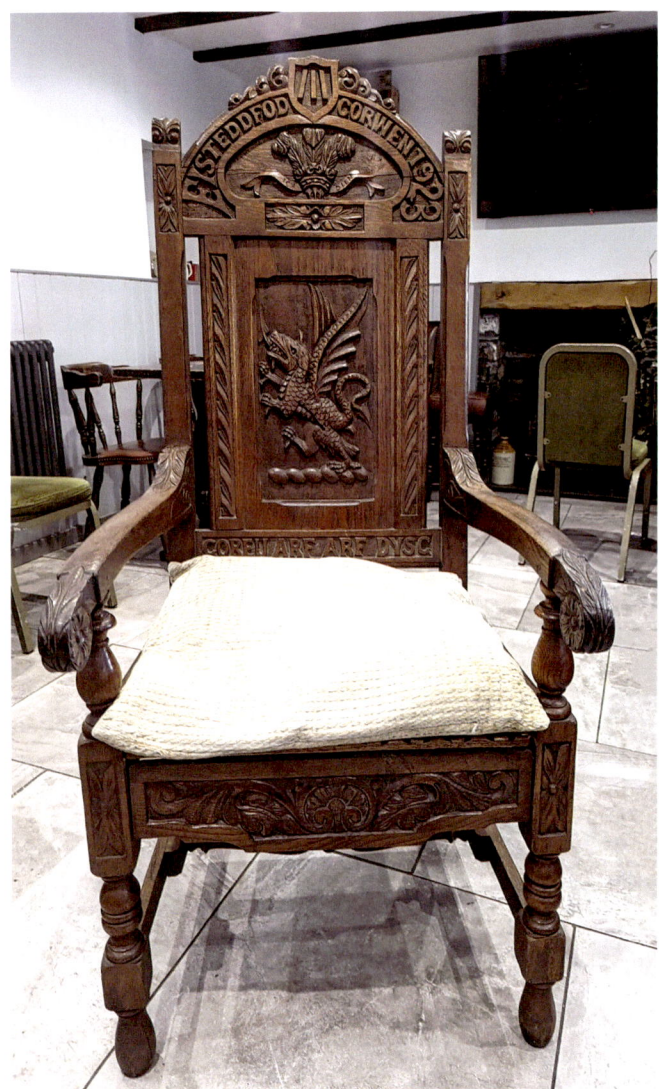

Eagle Inn, LLanfihangle-
ar-Arth.

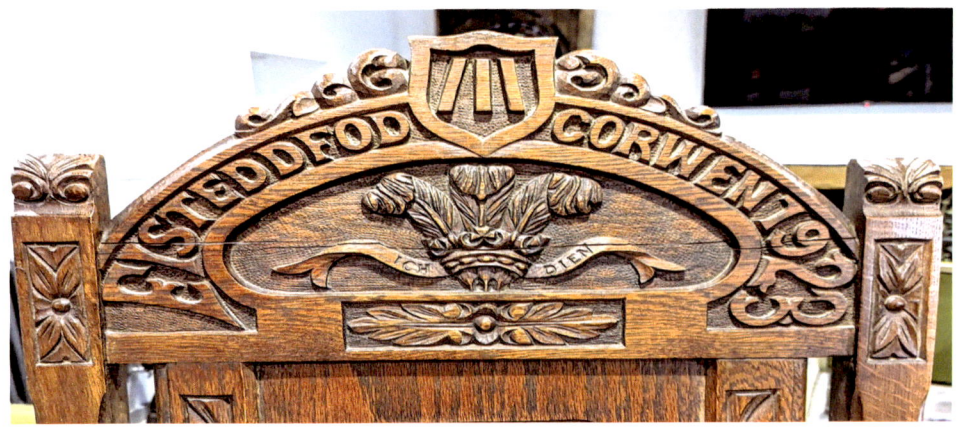

DID YOU KNOW?
Throughout the medieval period, high-backed chairs with arm rests were reserved for royalty, high-status military personnel, and religious and political leaders. Most ordinary people could only afford to make stools or benches until the 1700s. The award of an armchair immediately elevated the social class of a winning bard, with the prized chairs becoming much sought after.

After 1176 eisteddfodau were held locally throughout Wales under the patronage of Welsh gentry and noblemen, developing into grand folk festivals attracting thousands of visitors. The next documented eisteddfod took place in 1451 at Carmarthen Castle under the patronage of Gruffudd ap Nicolas, a nobleman and leading administrative figure in South Wales, known as 'The Eagle of Carmarthen'. The event lasted for three months and the prize for poetry was won by Dafydd ab Edmwnd, who was presented with a *cadair arian* (silver chair), which is said to have been fashioned by Gruffudd ap Nicolas himself. Controversy surrounded the eisteddfod when poet and priest Llawdden accused Gruffudd ap Nicolas of accepting a bribe from Dafydd ab Edmwnd in return for the silver chair.

The following year the eisteddfod was held in the grounds of the old St John's Priory, Carmarthen, and it was here that the rules for poetry and education were developed and agreed for the creation of bardic schools. Until this time the training of Welsh poets had always been a secret craft handed down from teacher to apprentice. As the poetry of the professional bards became increasingly more inexplicable, bards with humbler origins and less formal training began composing less complex and more popular works of Welsh poetry.

When Queen Elizabeth I attempted to govern the eisteddfodau through royal patronage it proved very unpopular. During the sixteenth and seventeenth centuries Welsh nobility had become increasingly anglicised and had stopped granting employment or hospitality to Welsh-language poets. Although the eisteddfod continued, these factors saw gatherings become more informal and less well attended. The meetings became known as the 'Assemblies of Rhymers' and were held in taverns, cemeteries, or inns. As a result, Welsh interest dwindled to such a point that just four people attended the 1620 eisteddfod in Glamorgan.

Eisteddfodau continued locally until attempts to revive the once prestigious event were made in 1819, when the first provincial eisteddfod was held in Carmarthen. This event was attended by Edward Williams, better known by his bardic name Iolo Morgannwg. He was the creator of the Gorsedd of Bards, a society of poets, writers, musicians, artists and individuals who contributed notably in preserving Welsh culture through the medium of the Welsh language. The word Gorsedd in Welsh means 'throne', and much of its ritual is based on the activities of ancient Celtic Druidism.

Iolo Morgannwg travelled to Carmarthen with a pocketful of chippings, and when he arrived traced the Gorsedd circle on the lawn of the Ivy Bush Inn. There he invested

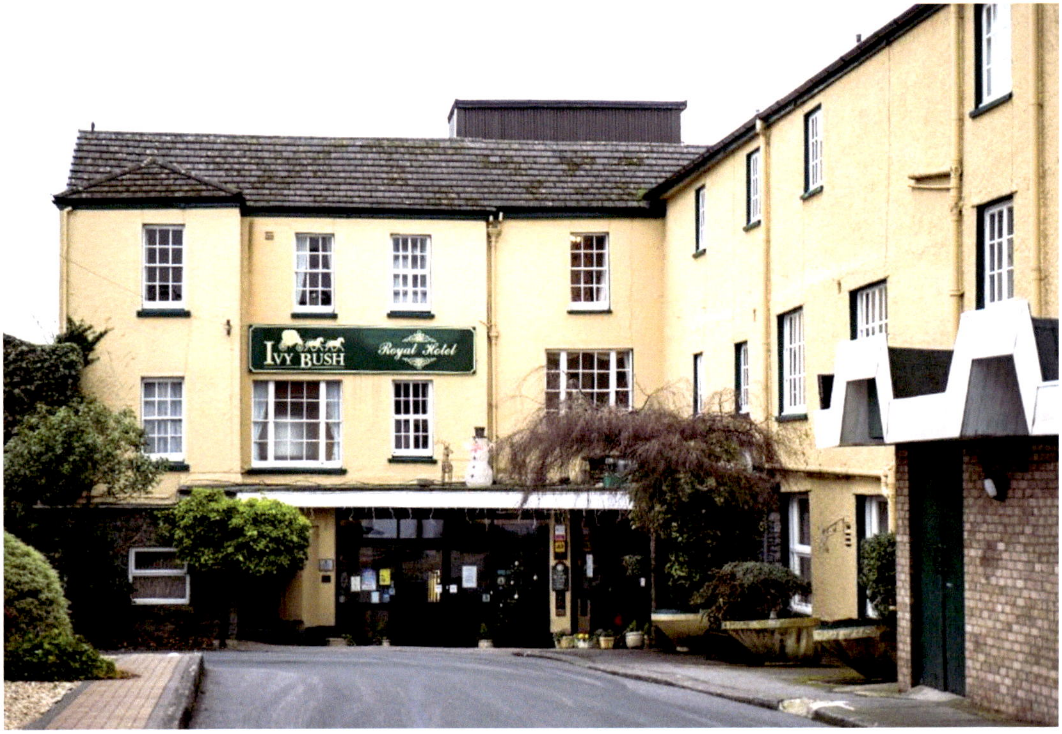

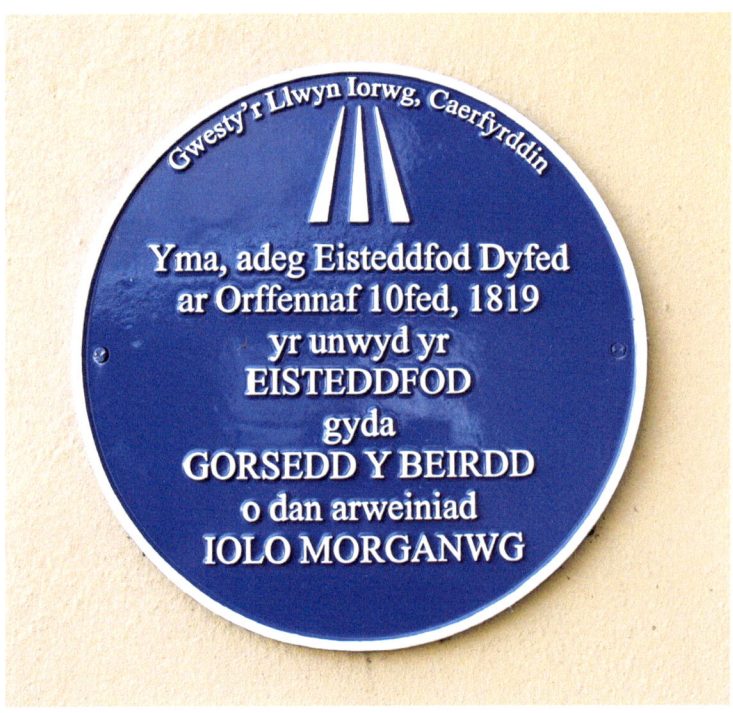

Former Ivy Bush Inn.

Gwesty'r Llwyn Iorwg, Caerfyrddin

Yma, adeg Eisteddfod Dyfed
ar Orffennaf 10fed, 1819
yr unwyd yr
EISTEDDFOD
gyda
GORSEDD Y BEIRDD
o dan arweiniad
IOLO MORGANWG

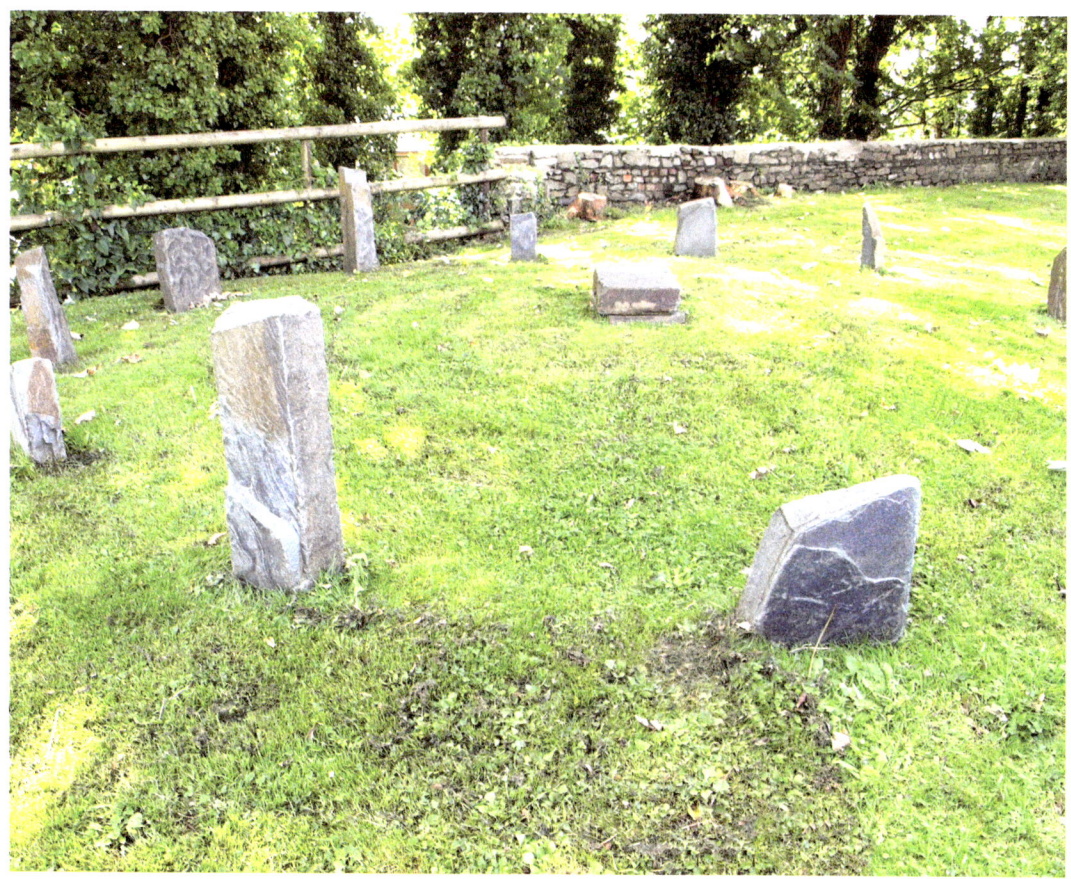

Garden of Ivy Bush Hotel.

bards and druids. Among them was the famous Bishop Thomas Burgess of St Davids, a great patron of the provincial eisteddfodau. Morgannwg inaugurated druids with a white ribbon to represent innocence, bards with a blue ribbon to represent truth, and Ovates with a green ribbon to represent the arts.

In 1880 the National Eisteddfod Association was formed to celebrate Welsh culture through literary, musical and dance competitions. Although the druidic Gorsedd was not initially included, today it plays an important part in the celebrations. Each annual festival is opened by a proclamation delivered from a cluster of standing stones known as the Gorsedd stones. Gorsedd stones are groups of standing stones constructed for the National Eisteddfod of Wales and form an essential part of the druidic Gorsedd ceremonies at the eisteddfod. The stones are arranged in a circle, usually forming twelve stone pillars. At the centre of the circle is the Maen Llog (Logan Stone), a large, flat-topped stone which is used as a platform. Carmarthen first hosted the event in 1911, then again in 1935 and most recently in 1974. Gorsedd stones were erected in the public park during 1973 for the 1974 eisteddfod and can be seen their today.

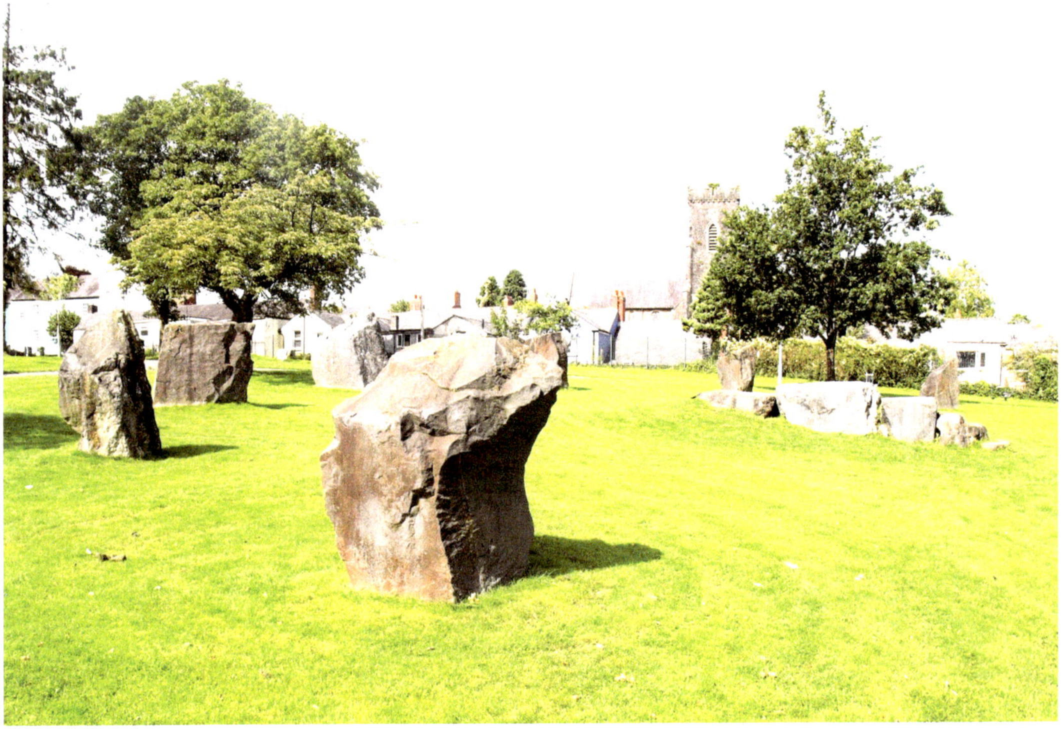

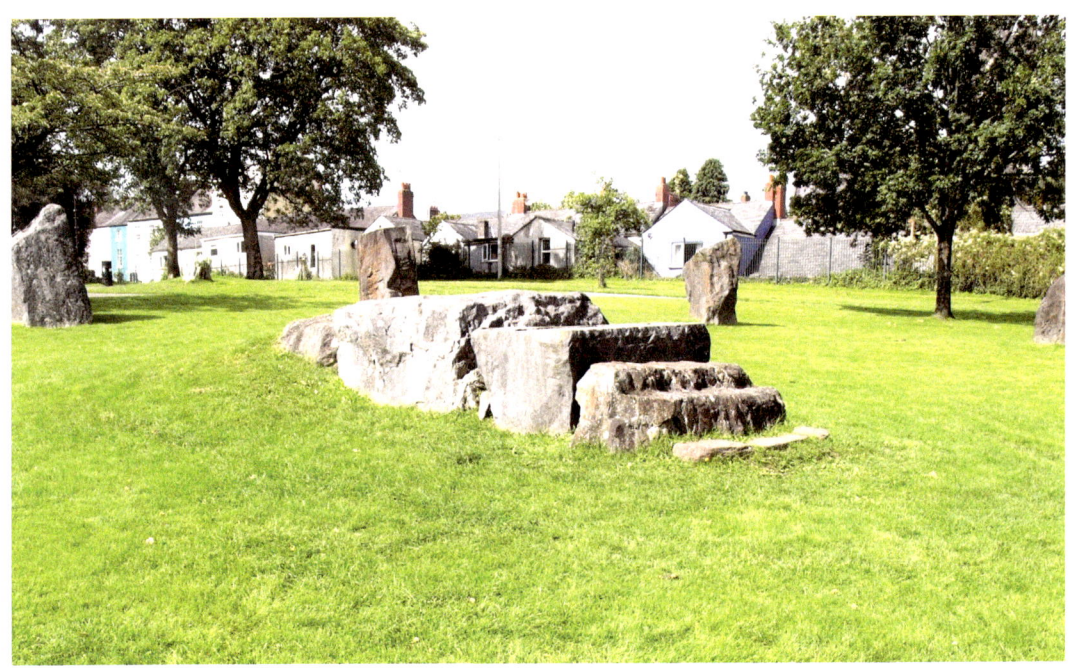

Gorsedd Stones, Carmarthen Park.

Gorsedd Stones, Carmarthen Park.

67

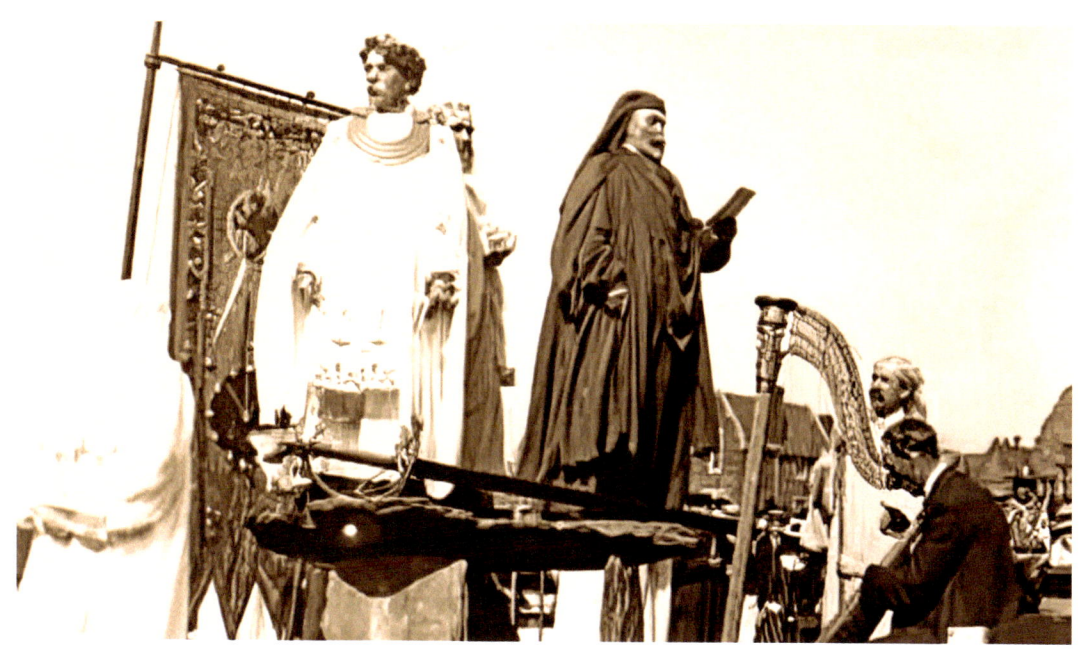

National Eisteddfod, 1911. (PD)

6. Pioneers of Enterprise and Endeavour

Carmarthen's past is filled with important firsts, noteworthy people, and heroic acts demonstrating initiative and effort. While the heroes, pioneers, and trailblazers highlighted in this chapter may not be as well known as the town's more established personalities, their influences on the town's history are no less significant.

Dorothea Bate was one of the few pioneering women in the forefront of science during the late nineteenth century but is often overlooked. She was born in 1878 in Napier House, Spilman Street. She had little formal education but was intrigued by wildlife. Her father was the town's Police Superintendent and when they moved to the Wye Valley in her early teens, she began exploring the caves. Among her first discoveries were fifteen different species of mammals and birds dating to the Ice Age.

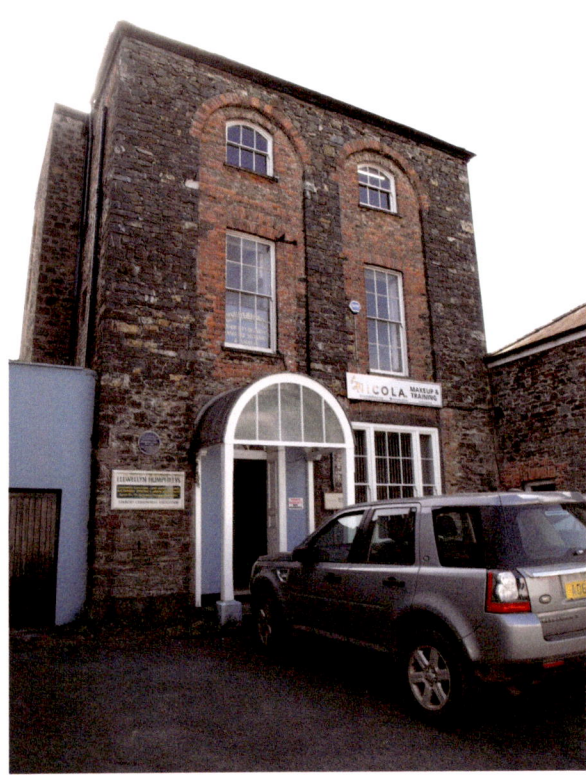

Napier House.

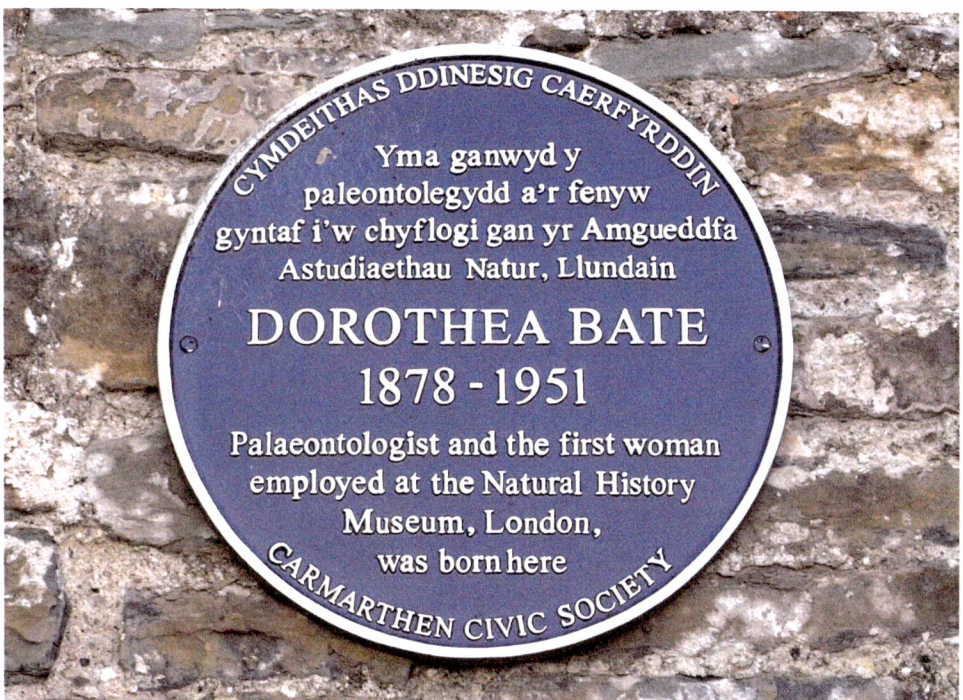

Aged nineteen, she travelled alone to the Natural History Museum (NHM), London, in search of employment. This was not in response to an advert, but due to her personal desire to become a natural history scientist. She had no idea there were no vacancies or women scientists employed at the museum. Women would only become official members of the scientific staff in 1928. The resolute Dorothea secured unofficial employment sorting bird skins in the Department of Zoology and later catalogued and prepared fossils for display and storage. She wasn't salaried but paid piecemeal for the number of specimens she prepared.

When she was twenty-two, NHM colleagues encouraged her to publish her first report about her findings on small-boned mammals. In 1901 she self-funded an eighteen-month expedition to Cyprus where she collected over 200 specimens of mammals, birds and insects. She won a grant from the Royal Society in 1902, which she used to discover a new species of dwarf elephant. She authored a scientific paper about her discovery, which the society published, and a reconstruction of the elephant was shown at the NHM in 1915.

Dorothea hired local guides to do the digging and when the only way she knew to get through a rock floor was to blast it open, she would use gunpowder or dynamite to go deeper. During 1904 Dorothea explored Crete and the Balearics often working with a high fever. She unearthed several extinct Mediterranean species, including a 1-metre-tall dwarf elephant, dwarf mammoths, and a bizarre mouse-goat.

Eventually Dorothea became the first female scientist employed at the NHM, where she remained for fifty years studying ornithology, palaeontology, geology and anatomy. She is also acknowledged as a trailblazer in archaeozoology, the study of remains of animals from archaeological sites.

Her life's work was to find fossils of recently extinct mammals and to understand how and why giant and dwarf lifeforms evolved. Between 1935 and 1937 she excavated in Palestine where she discovered many animals that were over 1.8 million years old, including elephants, tortoises, and a new species of horse.

In 1940 the Geological Society of London awarded Dorothea the Wollaston Fund for her published research. In the same year she was also elected a fellow of the Geological Society. The discoveries she made during her decades of exploration in the Mediterranean and Near East have left a lasting scientific legacy that is still considered valid today. By the end of her life Dorothea had published eighty scientific papers and written over a hundred unpublished works. She became Officer-in-Charge of the Tring Museum, Hertfordshire, an outpost of the NHM, until her death in January 1951, aged seventy-two. Today a blue plaque on the house in which she was born commemorates Dorothea and her achievements.

For a period during the late eighteenth century Carmarthen was at the centre of the Welsh book trade and home by birth or occupation to Wales's pioneer printers. It was also home to Wales's first permanent printing press. Isaac Carter's press first printed in 1718 at Adpar, Newcastle Emlyn, before moving to Carmarthen in 1725. Prior to that Welsh printing was produced in Shrewsbury or London.

Four years earlier Nicholas Thomas, a friend and patron of Carter, had set up the town's first printing press in 1721. In 1730 another printer, John Breden, opened a third press in the town. These three printing presses were the first to operate in Wales. Between 1721 and 1871 thirty-six companies had set up printing and publication businesses in the town, which became known as the Athens of Wales. Some of the most notable master printers are below.

John Ross was a Scotsman who learned to read and write Welsh and published more books during the eighteenth century in Welsh or relating to Wales than all the other printers in Wales combined. He printed three editions of the Welsh Bible known as the 'Peter Williams Bible'. Following his death in 1807, his daughter Ann continued the business until she died in 1842 aged 107. In his honour the town named Ross Avenue after him and mounted a blue plaque on the Capel Yr Annibynwyr, in Lammas Street.

Ann and another female printer, Hannah White, were the town's only female printers in this era. Hannah, with her sons, traded as H. White and Sons, printers, booksellers and stationers until her death, aged eighty, in 1861.

The most skilled of the early pioneer printers was John Ross's apprentice John Daniel. Daniel, a Carmarthen man born and bred, printed the Welsh Bible, an English to Welsh dictionary and was the first printer to produce printed music in staff notation.

William Spurrell, noted as an outstanding printer, was born at No. 13 Quay Street, and studied at the Queen Elizabeth Grammar School. Following his apprenticeship under master printer John Powell Davies, he worked for a printing firm in London, before returning to Carmarthen in 1840 to open his printing works. William produced many books, including a dictionary of the Welsh and English languages, an English-Welsh dictionary, and several Welsh grammar books. In addition to writing and publishing *Carmarthen and its Neighbourhood* and many other Welsh language books, William also designed the standard typecase used by all printers today.

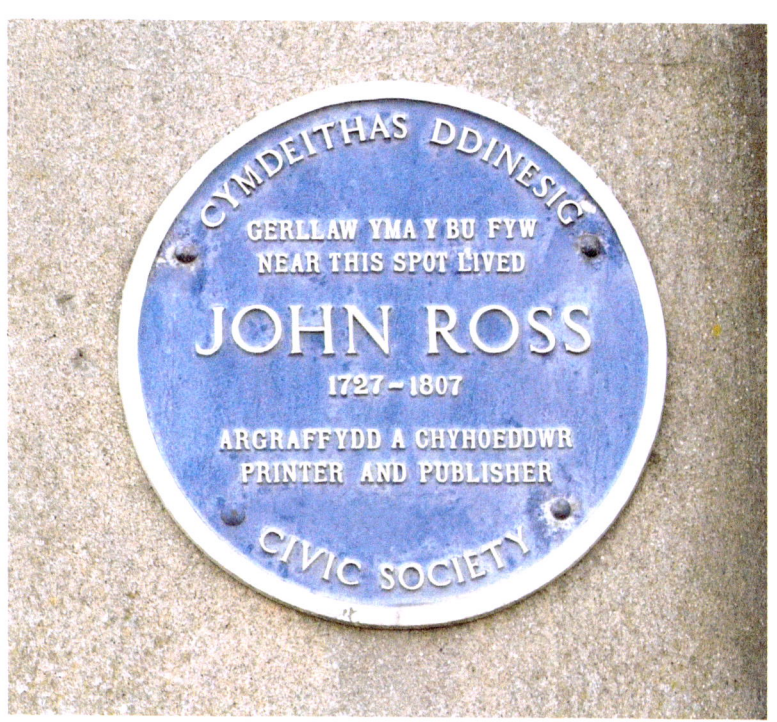

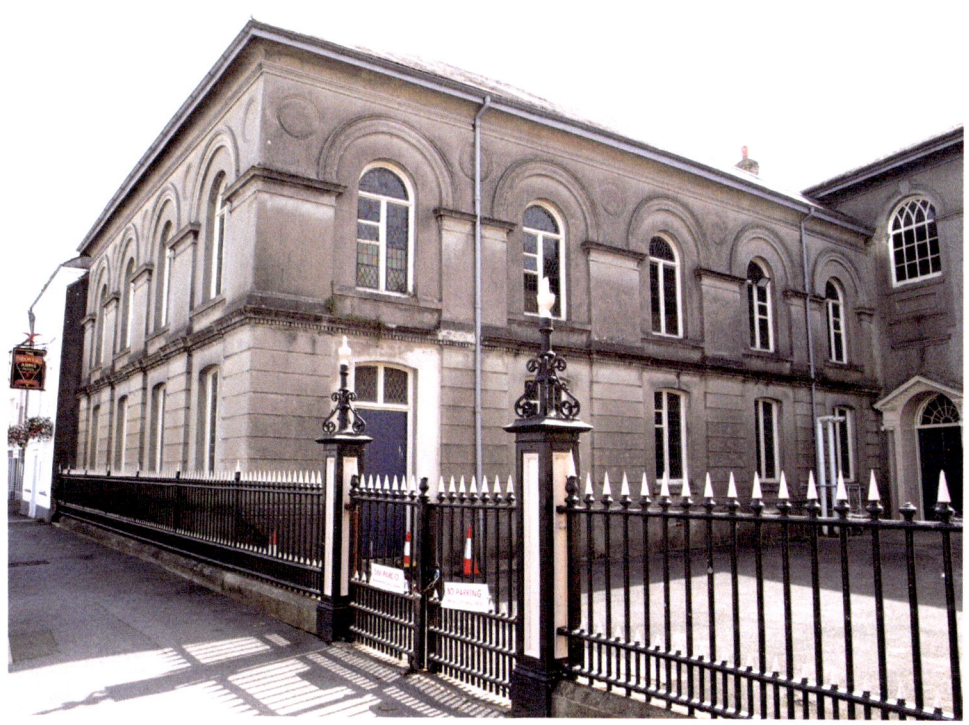

Capel Yr Annibynwyr.

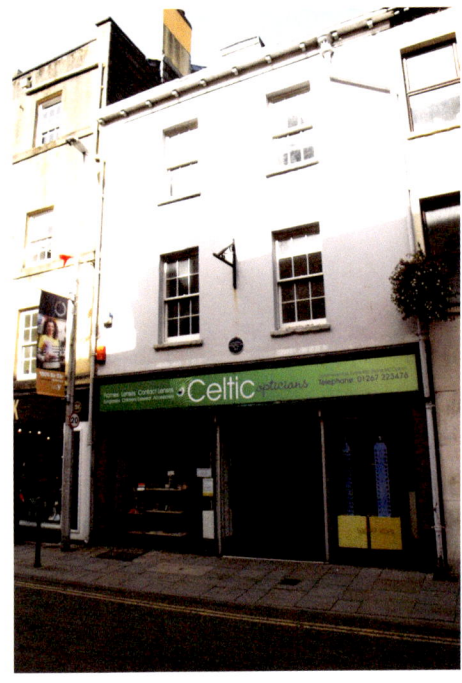

King Street.

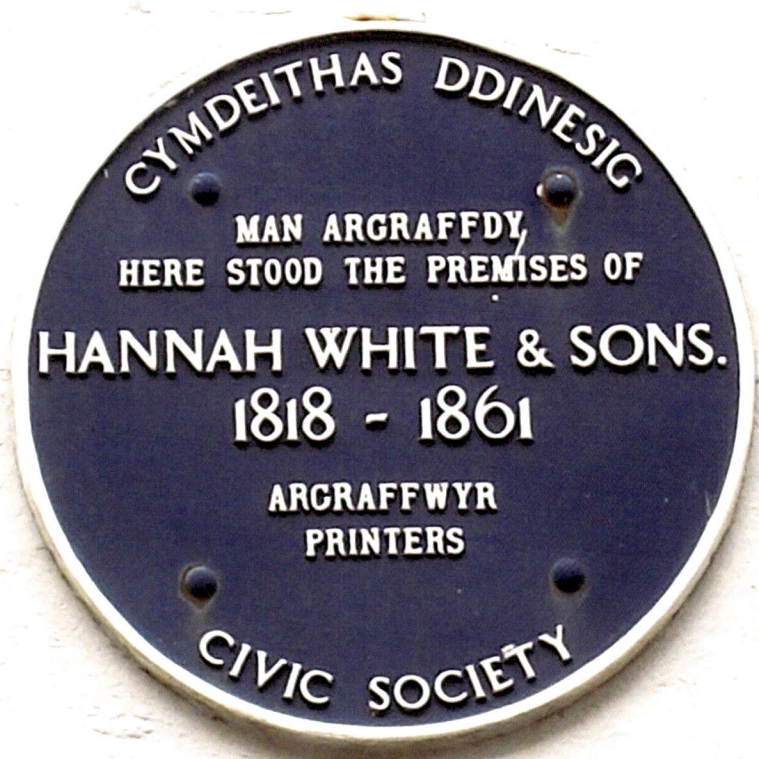

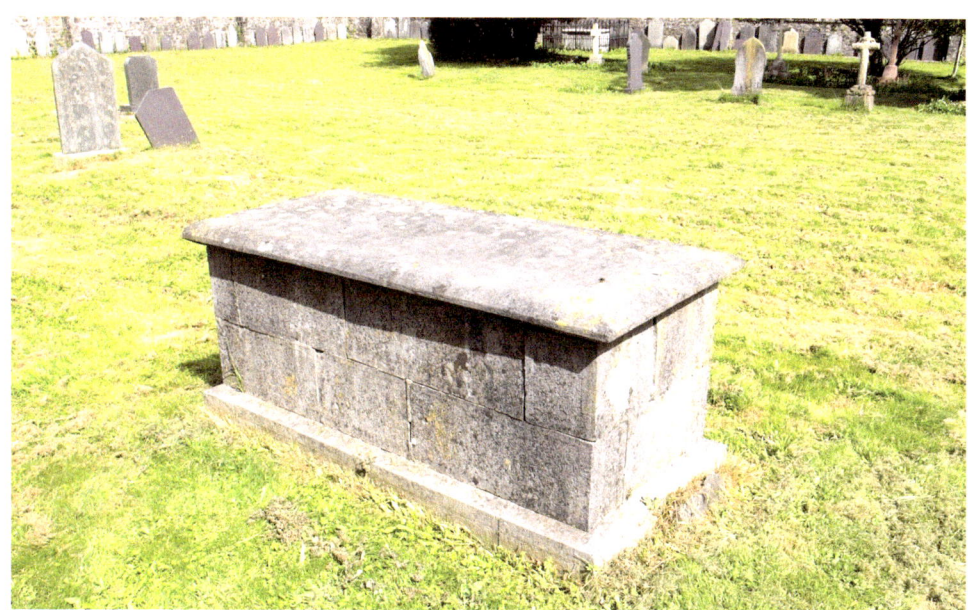

Above: Hannah White's grave,
St David's.

Right: William Spurrell's
grave, St David's.

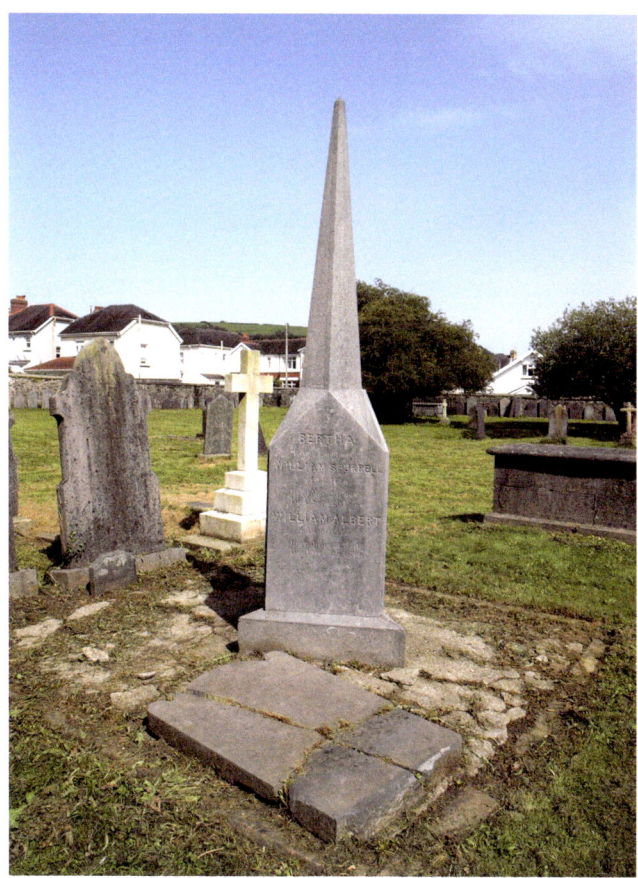

7. Civic Pride and the Establishment of Education

A Tale of Two Towns

When the Normans arrived in Carmarthen, they created a new town (New Carmarthen) in the shadow of their castle, enclosing it within a protective wall. In time it became an important military location and commercial centre, which the Normans made a borough with all the privileges that offered. The original Welsh town of Carmarthen, on the site of the old Roman town, became known as Old Carmarthen Town. With the Welsh always ready to overthrow the English, demands made by the Normans for ships, provisions and weapons to support the king's wars abroad often led to violent clashes between the two towns.

The Normans, with their charters and royal privileges, resented Welsh claims for parity of treatment and autonomy to hold their own markets, fairs and courts. Slowly, Old Carmarthen was granted privileges and charters that allowed it some autonomy. Yet it wasn't until 1546, following the dissolution of the priory and the friary during the Reformation, that Henry VIII issued a charter joining the old town to the new. The two towns were unified to become a Corporate Borough known as Carmarthen Town with the power to have a common council and mayor.

Henry appointed a mayor and two bailiffs and a common council of twenty citizens and twenty burgesses. A new charter was issued by King James I in 1604, which elevated the status of the town from a borough to a county borough, making Carmarthen a county with the formal title 'The County and Borough of Carmarthen'. The charter granted the right for Carmarthen to replace their two existing bailiffs with two sheriffs.

In 1764 King George III set up a new charter that named Carmarthen 'Our Borough of Carmarthen', returning it to borough status with a governing borough council. Over the centuries various charters and Acts of Parliament have seen the size and name of the borough change several times with a decrease in the number of council members and their responsibilities.

The Local Government Reforms Act of 1835 reduced the number of sheriffs in boroughs across the UK. In Carmarthen, the number went from two to one, with their office and duties becoming mostly ceremonial. Many boroughs lost their sheriff's office, which was never replaced. Carmarthen is unique as it is one of only two towns in Wales to have a sheriff – the other is Haverfordwest. The Sheriff of Carmarthen usually assumes office as part of a three-year pledge to serve the town as sheriff, deputy mayor and lastly as mayor.

DID YOU KNOW?

In 1485 Richard III became the last King of England to die on a battlefield. He was killed by Sir Rhys ap Thomas, Mayor of Carmarthen between 1488 and 1489. Rhys initially swore fidelity to Richard, but Henry Tudor offered a better deal. Rhys pursued Richard at Bosworth Field and used a halberd (a two-handed pole weapon) to deliver a fatal blow to the back of his head. This act and his support of Henry ensured Rhys's status as one of the most influential men in Tudor Wales.

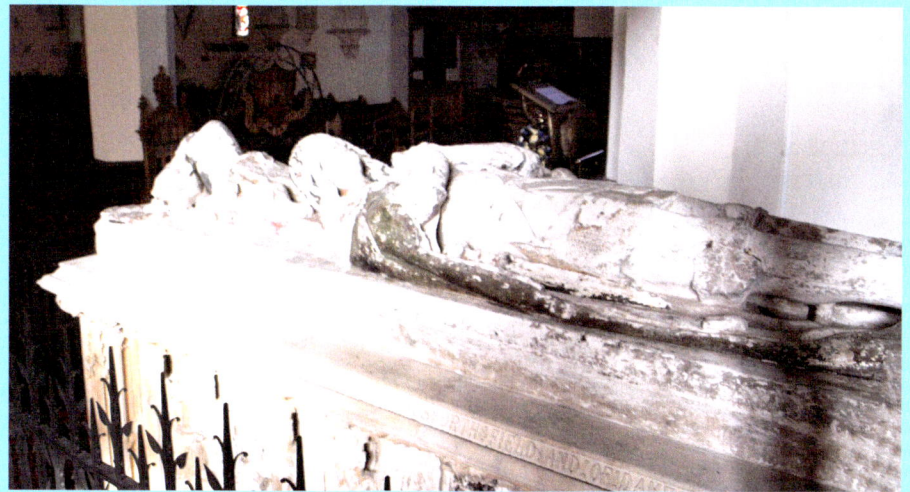

Tomb of Sir Rhys ap Thomas.

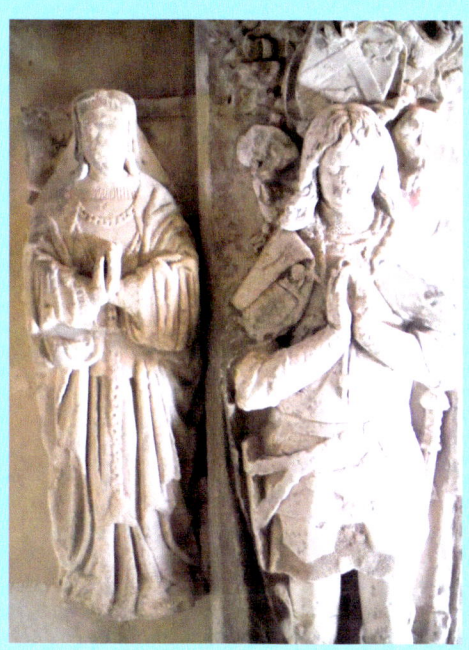

Tomb of Sir Rhys ap Thomas.

The Corporation regalia is a vestige of Carmarthen's civic past that may still be seen today. The State Sword, gifted via royal grant by King Henry VIII in 1546, is among them. The bejewelled sword of Castilian steel was a token of his appreciation for the town's services to him. Thus, Carmarthen became, and is still, the only town in Wales to have the privilege of having a sword carried before the mayor on state occasions.

The sword is reversed to form a cross when it enters a church, and in times of conflict when Britain is at war, the sword can be carried unsheathed by the mayor until peace is

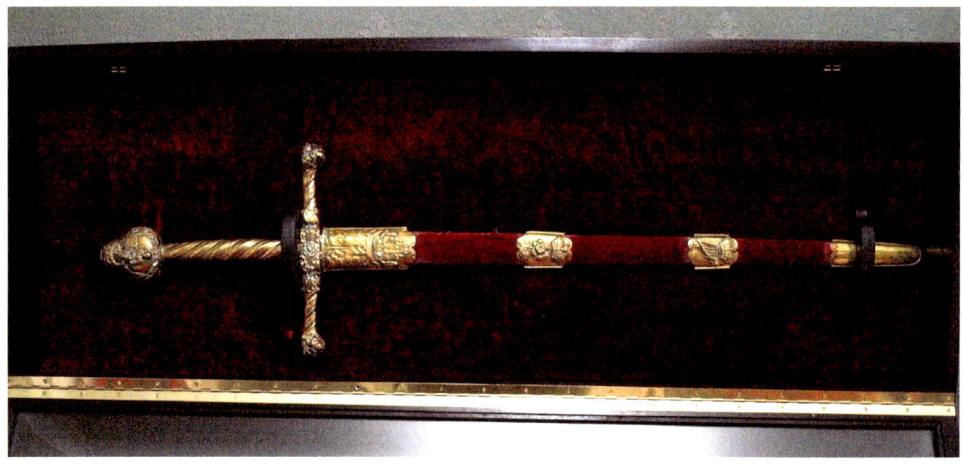

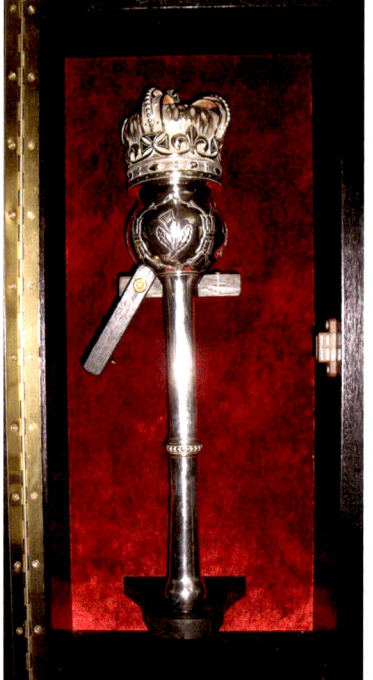

Above: The State Sword.

Left: One of the maces.

declared. Among the other corporation regalia are two silver maces and the bellman's staff. An unusual item of corporation regalia is the silver oar, an 18-inch symbol of the mayor's office as Admiral of the Port of Carmarthen.

The current borough coat of arms was granted to the town in 1936 and was created to mirror the borough's original sixteenth-century seal. The central portion of the crest is based on the original seal, the coracle, a light rowing boat made of leather and trellis; the figure of a man is a modern addition. An interesting detail is the position of the two birds, traditionally regarded as the ravens of Sir Rhys ap Thomas, but now officially described as Cornish choughs. On the State Sword and mayor's chain they face outwards, while on the maces and coat of arms, they face inwards.

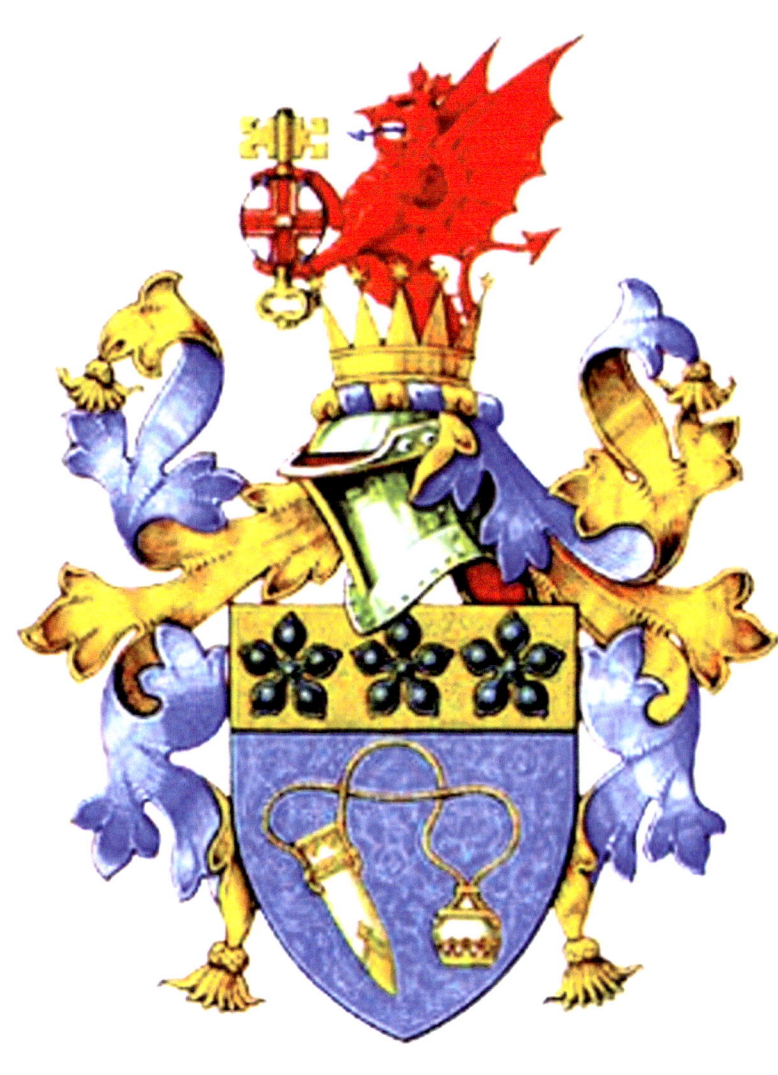

Borough coat
of arms. (PD)

It's hard to imagine, given the turmoil, lawlessness, and troublesome times, briefly covered in earlier chapters, that beating at the centre of Carmarthen's cultural heart were several distinguished and well-respected educational establishments. While many of their alumni have in their time shaped and influenced Welsh history, their stories, like their influence, have become less well known with the passing of time but are still noteworthy.

The University of Wales Trinity St David is the oldest surviving teacher training college in Wales. It opened in Carmarthen in 1848 as the South Wales and Monmouthshire Training College and its first students were twenty-two men destined to become teachers in elementary schools. Women were not admitted until 1957 for fear they might divert the men from their studies.

Carmarthen's Presbyterian College was built in 1840 to train students for the Nonconformist ministry. Two years later it was affiliated with the University of London to become the first institution in Wales offering training for a university degree and was open to students of all denominations. The college closed in 1963. After this the building was used as office accommodation before it became the Carmarthen Evangelical Church.

The Queen Elizabeth Grammar School for boys is one of the oldest and most celebrated grammar schools in Wales. Founded in 1576 for 'the education of and

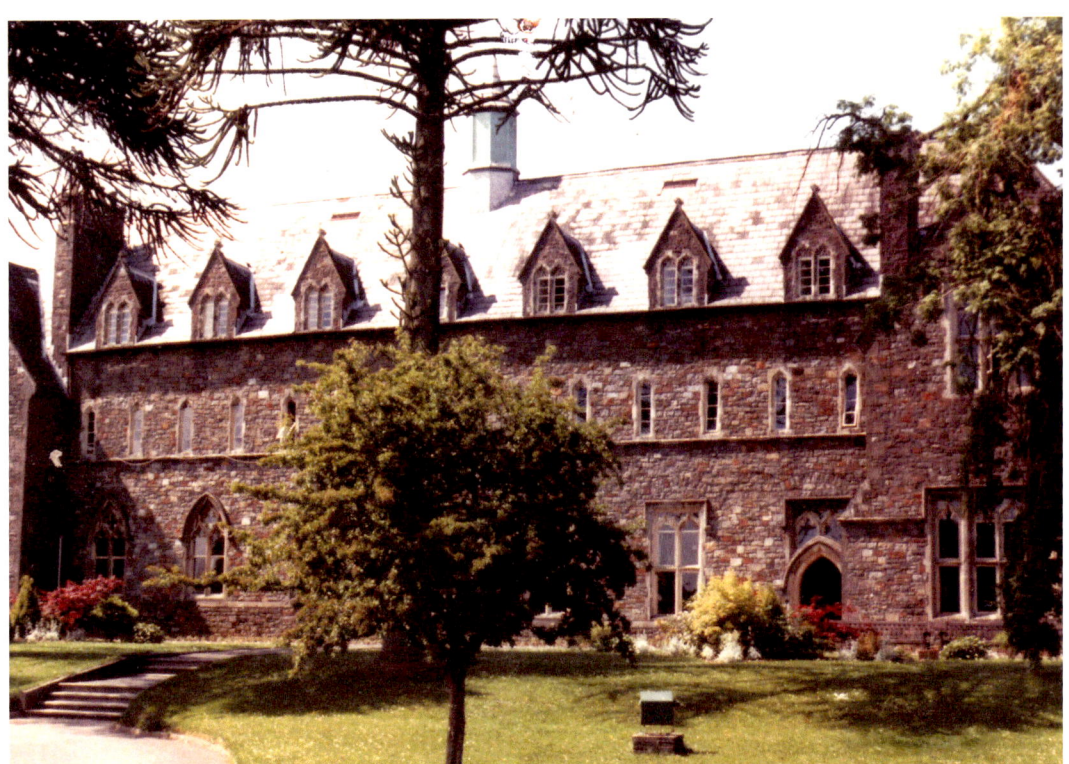

Old building of Trinity College.

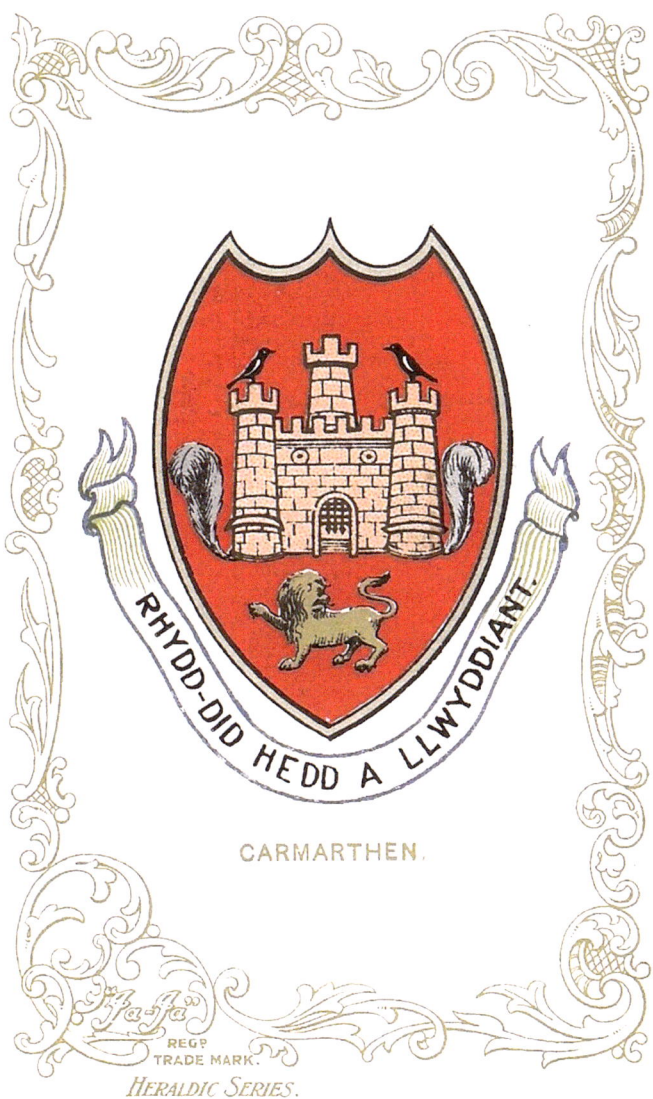

CARMARTHEN.

RHYDD-DID HEDD A LLWYDDIANT

Trinity College coat of arms. (PD)

instruction of boys in grammar and other inferior books', it was originally situated in Priory Street. In 1857 the school merged with Sir Thomas Powell's Charity School, built in 1729 for the instruction of six poor boys. Over its years the school grew to accommodate fifteen free places and thirty-four paying scholars. The two schools became known as the 'Endowed Schools' and moved to a new site above Richmond Terrace in 1884, later becoming a secondary school. The school closed in 1978. Today the building exists as a four-house conversion, with a plaque at the entrance to Parc Myrddin commemorating the school.

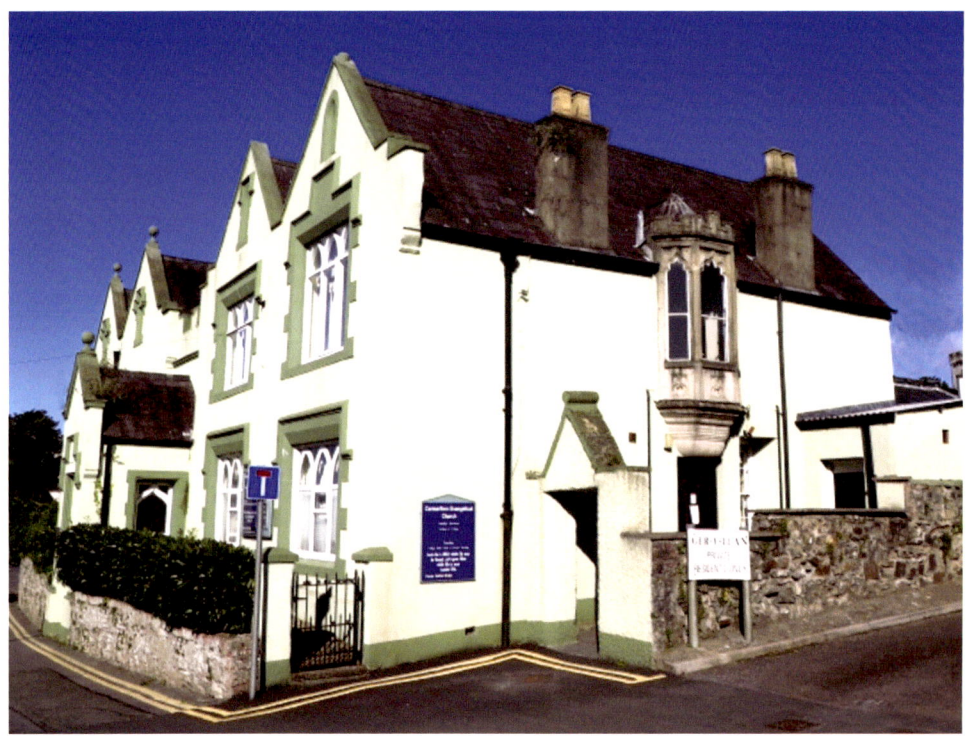

Former Presbyterian College.

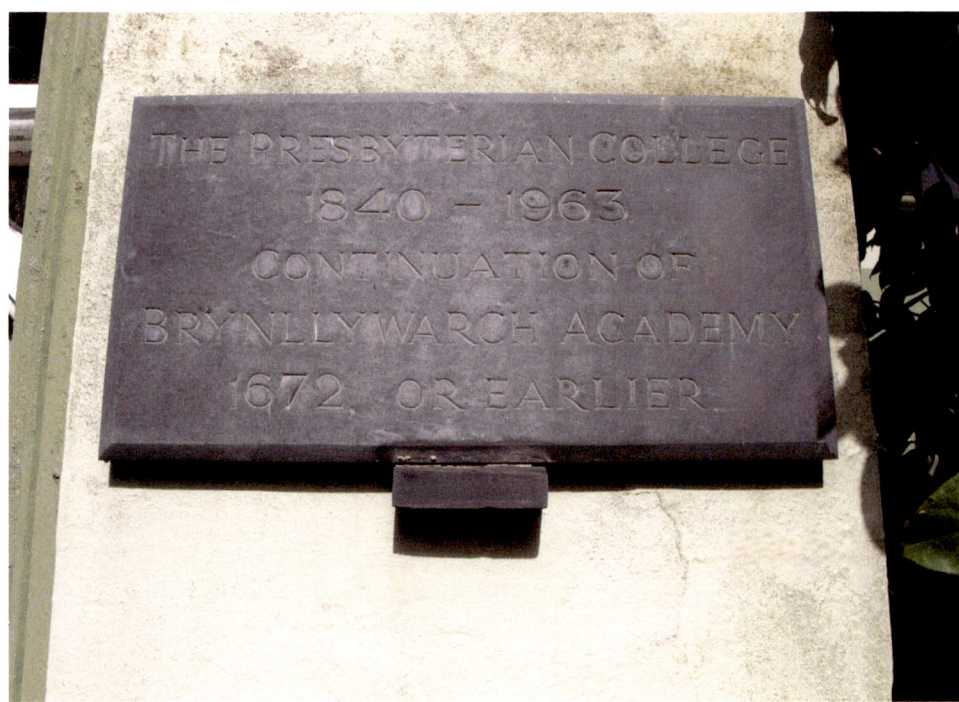

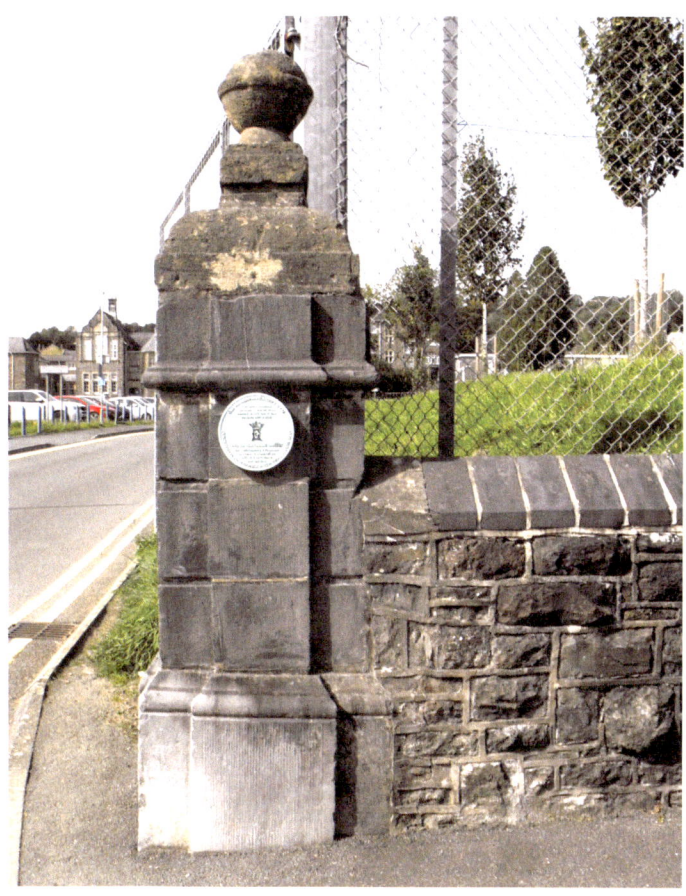

Entrance to Parc Myrddin.

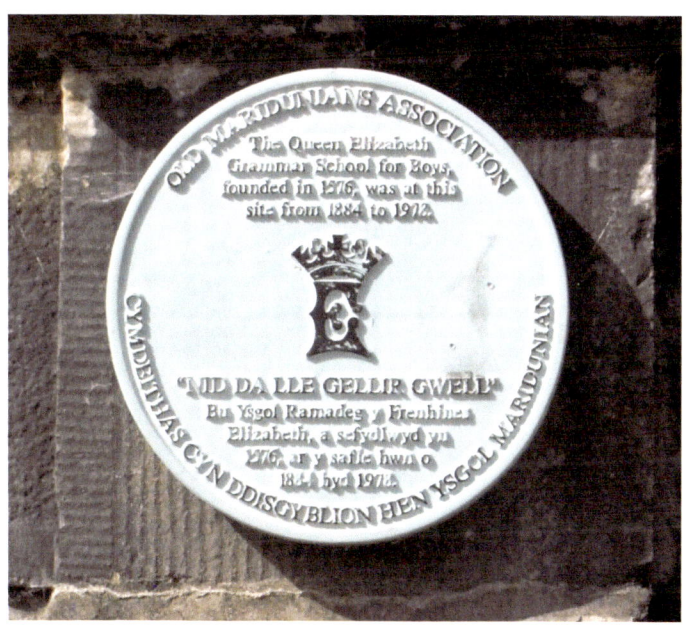

8. Some More Firsts and a Few Lasts

In 1837 the Carmarthen Poor Law Union was formed to provide a place where people unable to support themselves could live and work. In the same year, the Penlan Union Workhouse was built on Penlan Road to accommodate 140 inmates. Conditions in the workhouses were deliberately made harsh and degrading to deter all but the destitute. On 19 June 1843, the workhouse was stormed by the 'Rebecca Rioters', who forced the matron to hand over his keys and smashed windows and furniture before besieging the workhouse. When the 4th Light Dragoons arrived, a section dismounted, fixed bayonets, and fired at the rioters inside before initiating a bayonet charge to remove them.

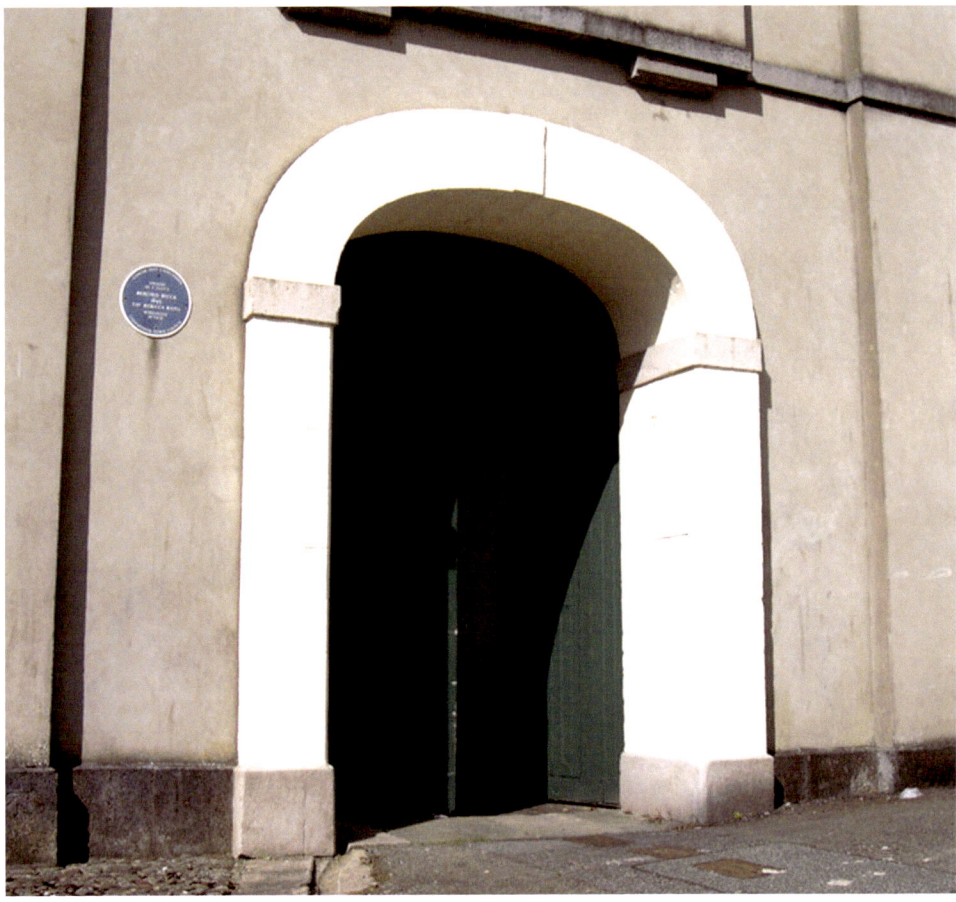

Entrance to Union Workhouse. (© John Duckfield)

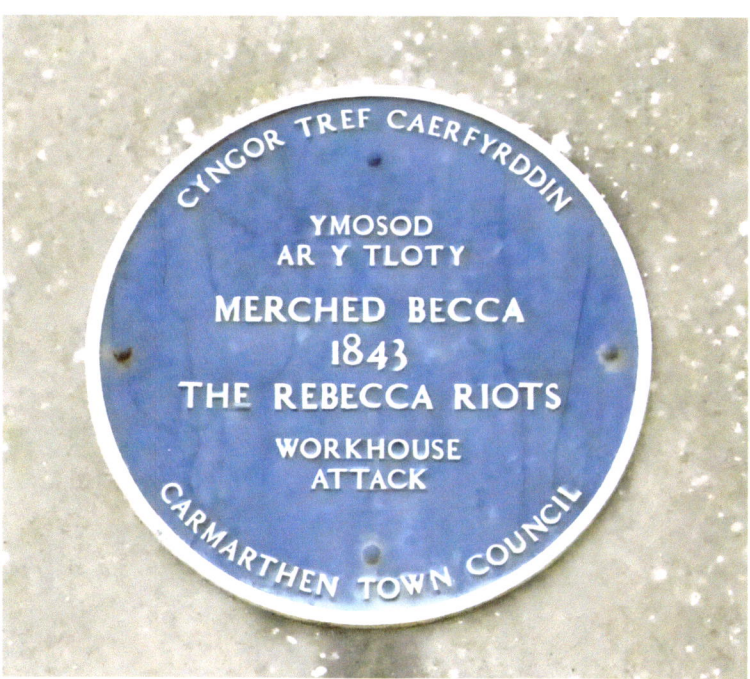

The rest of the mounted dragoons, sabres drawn, charged down around 2,000 rioters who were amassing in Waterloo Terrace. While there were no fatalities many people were injured and over sixty protesters arrested. Many of the men of the 4th Light Dragoons involved in the Carmarthen charge also took part in the Crimean War's infamous 'Charge of the Light Brigade' on 25 October 1854. Among those men to take part in both charges was Carmarthen-born David Thomas.

DID YOU KNOW?
The charge by the 4th Light Dragoons at Carmarthen in 1843 was the scene of the last cavalry charge by the British Army on mainland Britain. It was undertaken in response to social unrest caused by the excessive charges levied by tollgates and the intolerable conditions of institutions such as the workhouses. Known as the Rebecca Riots, men disguised themselves in women's clothes when they attacked tollgates and tollhouses.

David Thomas fought at the Battle of the Alma (20 September 1854) and the Battle of Inkerman (5 November 1854) and served through the Siege of Sebastopol (October 1854–September 1855). He earned three medals: the Crimean medal with four clasps, the Turkish medal, and a medal for distinguished service in the field. During the 'Charge of the Light Brigade,' David bravely fought through the Russian lines to reach a seriously injured officer, and, under heavy enemy fire, carried him back to British lines. Thomas's act of valour was remembered by the officer who, until his death many years later, sent him money during his retirement in Carmarthen. When that money stopped, ironically, Thomas was forced to seek refuge in the Penlan Union Workhouse, where he lived in poverty until his death, aged sixty-eight, in 1890.

Although Thomas was buried with full military honours at St David's Church, it wasn't until his death that the town realised it had lost another hero. A collection was six shillings short of the full cost of the funeral, and the missing money had to be produced by a reluctant relative.

DID YOU KNOW?
In the early eighteenth century in Carmarthen, it was customary for a hand bell to be rung in front of a funeral cortege as it continued through the streets of the town. The bell allowed people to line the route and pay their respect. Shops pulled down blinds and stopped serving until the cortege had passed and the bell had stopped ringing.

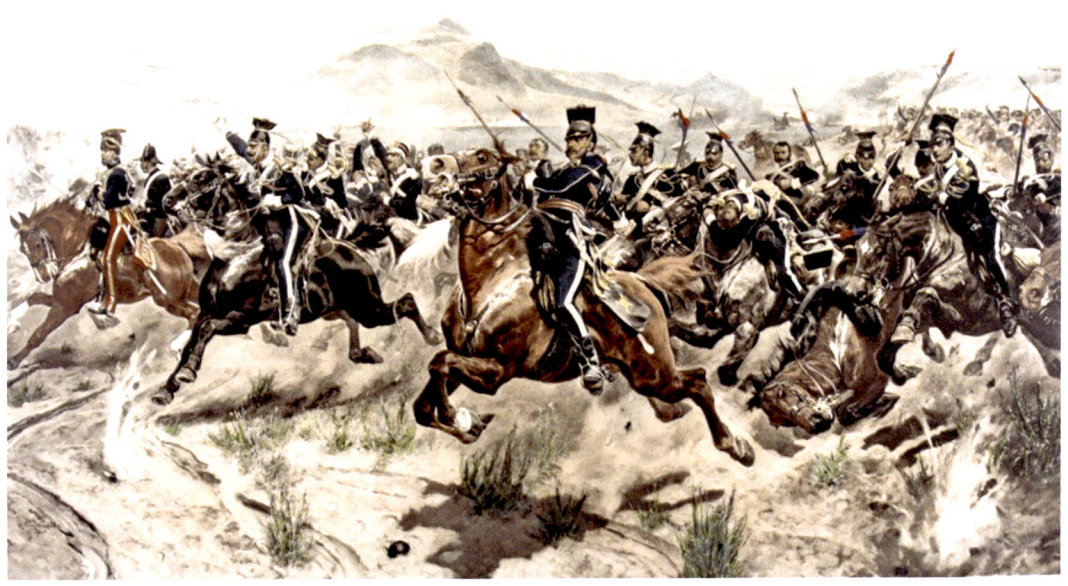

The Charge of the Light Brigade. (RCW)

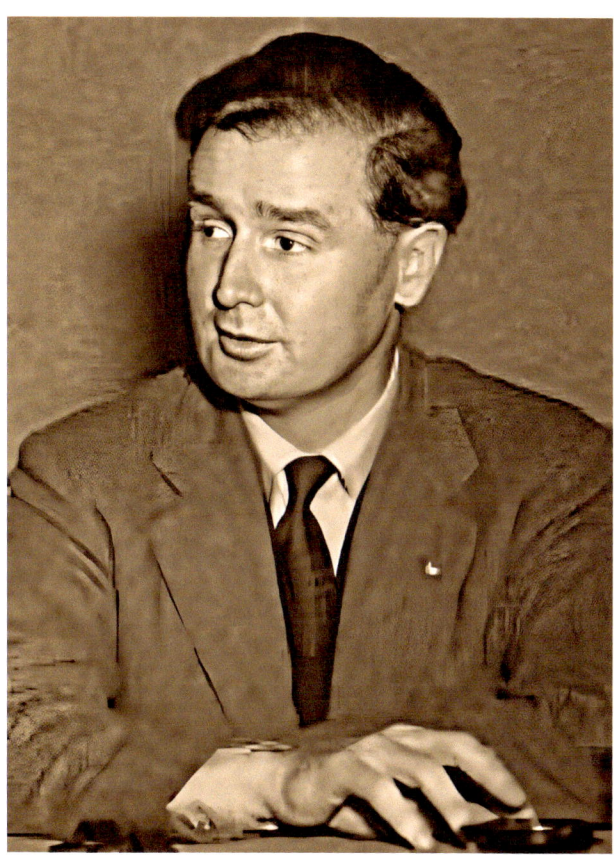

Gwynfor Evans. (© Geoff Charles)

According to Bailey's Records of Longevity, the oldest man in Carmarthen was Evan Williams, also an inmate at the Penlan Union Workhouse, who died in 1781 aged 145.

Another unsung Welsh hero linked to Carmarthen is Gwynfor Evans, born in 1912. Gwynfor was a politician, lawyer and author. A pacifist, he refused to fight during the Second World War and in 1945 he became President of Plaid Cymru, a position he held for thirty-six years. Notably Gwynfor opposed the British government's support of the Nigerian government in the civil war against Biafra (1967–70) and opposed the Vietnam War (1955–75).

In 1966, against all the odds, Gwynfor Evans won a thrilling victory at a parliamentary by-election in Carmarthen to become the first Member of Parliament to represent Plaid Cymru at Westminster. On election night, thousands of supporters packed Guildhall Square to chant his name and the event was even reported in *The New York Times*. He sat from 1966 to 1970, and again from 1974 to 1979. This was Plaid Cymru's first seat in Parliament and set Wales on the political path it travels today. A year later in 1967 the Labour government passed the first Welsh Language Act. Gwynfor is renowned for his part in the campaign to set up a Welsh language TV channel after Prime Minister Margaret Thatcher broke her party's manifesto promise to establish the channel. It spurred a widespread campaign of civil disobedience, which saw a number of people

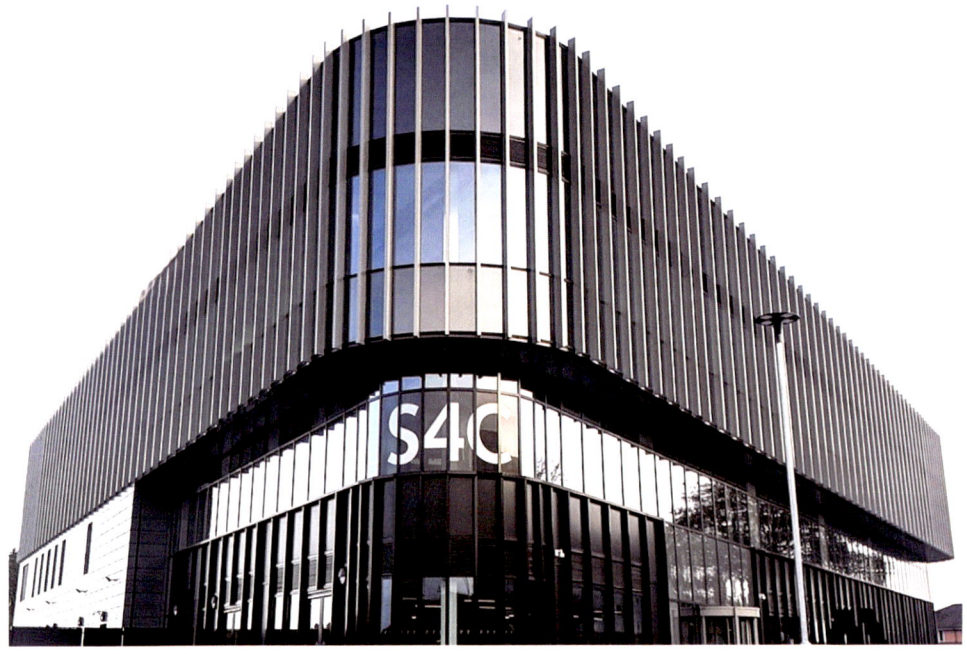

S4C Studios.

imprisoned, including several who appeared in Carmarthen Crown Court. The campaign culminated in 1980 when Gwynfor threatened to starve himself to death, forcing the 'Iron Lady' into an historic U-turn. S4C was established and its HQ is now in Carmarthen. Gwynfor died in 2005, aged ninety-two, after a lifetime of tireless campaigning on matters relating to language and cultural identity.

Lady Megan Lloyd George was the daughter of David Lloyd George, the only Welshman to become prime minister. She became the first woman MP in Wales, defecting from the Liberals to the Labour Party in 1955, where she won and held the Carmarthen seat from 1957 to 1966. A Welsh patriot, she was elected a bard of the National Eisteddfod in 1935 and became the first woman member of the Welsh church commissioners in 1942. Megan was the founding president of the 'Parliament for Wales' campaign.

In 1944 Megan opened the first Welsh Day debate at Westminster and was prominent among those who advocated for the Welsh Office and for the post of Secretary of State for Wales in the early 1960s. After winning Carmarthen for Labour in 1957 Megan returned to Parliament, remaining an MP until her death nine years later, aged sixty-four. An enthusiastic, radical and eloquent orator, she never failed to fight for policies beneficial to Wales. Megan was included in Walesonline's top fifty greatest Welsh men and women of all time in 2016.

Carmarthen's sporting and leisure connections date back to the time of the Romans and the construction of the impressive Moridunum Amphitheatre, built to host gladiatorial contests and celebrate religious holidays and events. Its seating area was 92 by 67 metres and its central arena of 46 by 27 metres, making it the most westerly amphitheatre in

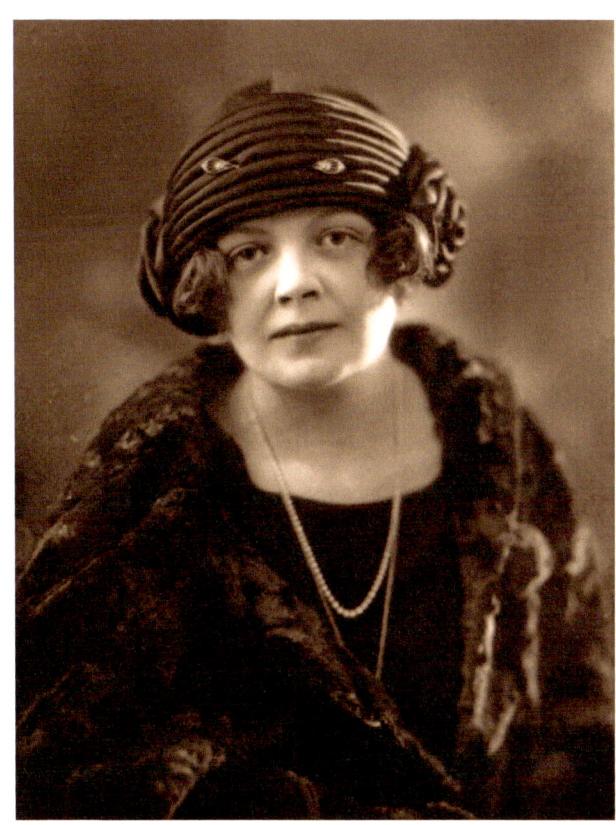

Right: Lady Megan Lloyd George.
(© Bassano Ltd)

Below: Moridunum
Amphitheatre.

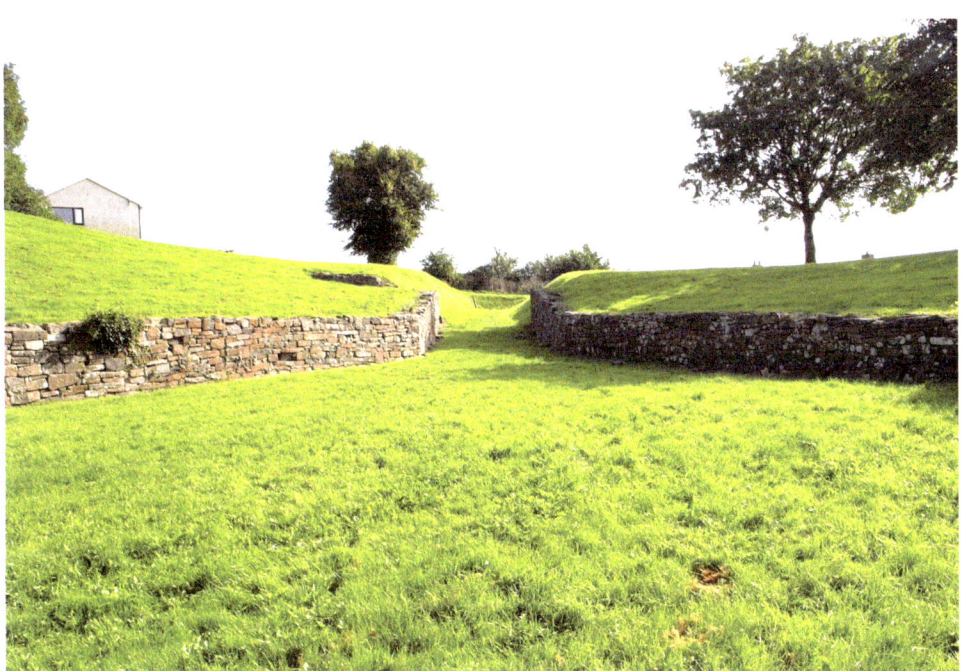

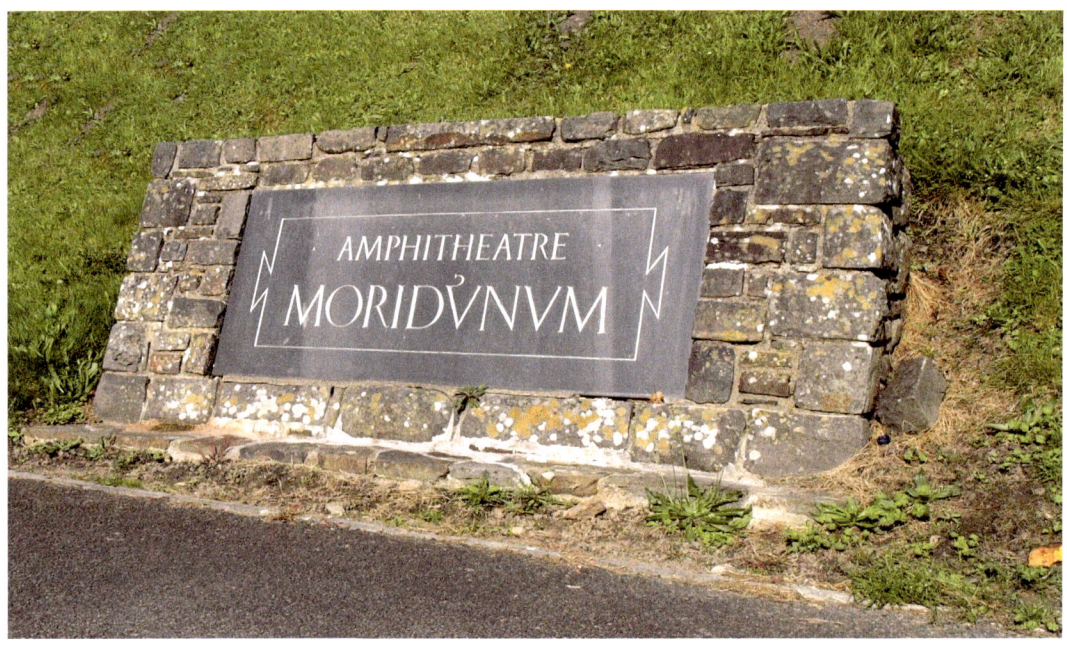

the Roman world, and one of only seven surviving amphitheatres in the UK. Part of it is preserved and openly accessible off Priory Street.

It is not well known that the town has a historic connection with cricket. In 1136 Geoffrey of Monmouth wrote his *History of the Kings of Britain* in which he included an account of Vortigern, King of the Britons, scouring the lands for Merlin during the sixth century. When his searchers arrived at the gates of Carmarthen, they reported seeing children playing an unusual game with a bat and ball. Historian Hadrian Allcroft's *The Origins of Cricket* positively establishes the game observed being played at Carmarthen as the origins of what we call cricket today.

One of the oldest sporting events to be played in Carmarthen was an early form of football called 'Cnapan.' In 1603 Welsh antiquarian George Owen wrote about how the ancient Britons played the game to improve their strength and stamina. Originally used as a form of military training in ancient times, it developed over time into a competitive sport.

The game was played between villages or districts, with as many as 2,000 people competing, including horsemen. On festival days teams would compete to move a greased wooden ball over several miles of countryside towards a goal, usually the church porch in an opponent's village. The ball was dropped an equal distance from the two goals and the 'pitch' included all the land in between. Players could kick, throw, or run with the ball, but it was mostly taken by hand. The rough nature of the game resulted in many injuries and participants were often killed, trampled underfoot, crushed in the crowd, or thrown from their horses.

Cnapan developed into the sport of rugby we see today. Carmarthen has two rugby clubs. Carmarthen Quins, formed in 1875, is a feeder club for Llanelli Scarlets and has

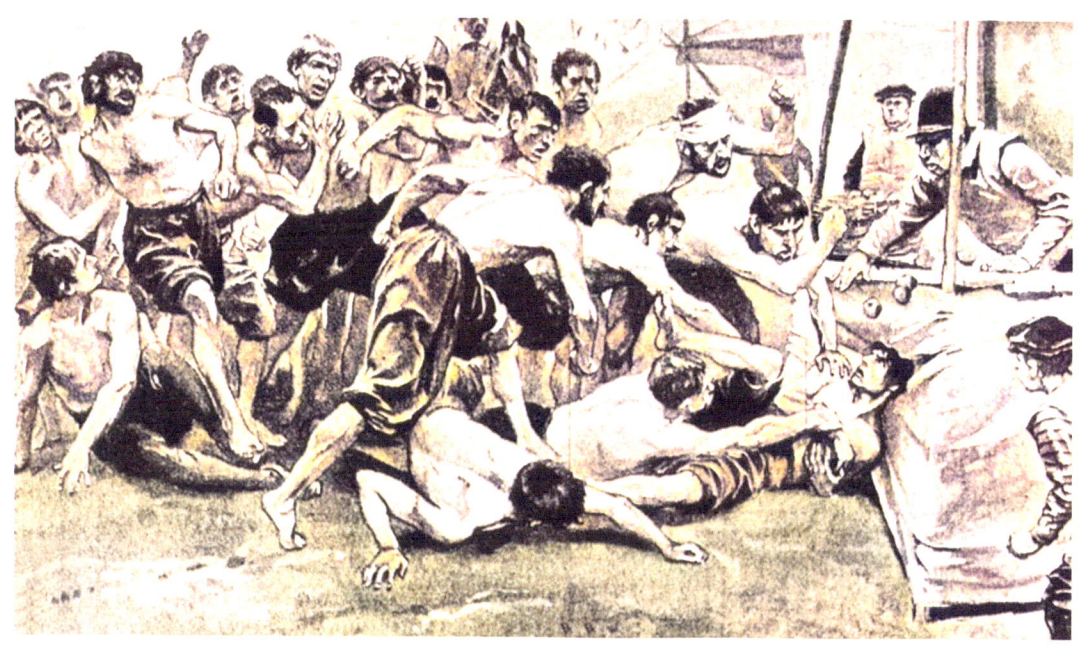

Depiction of Cnapan. (HMB)

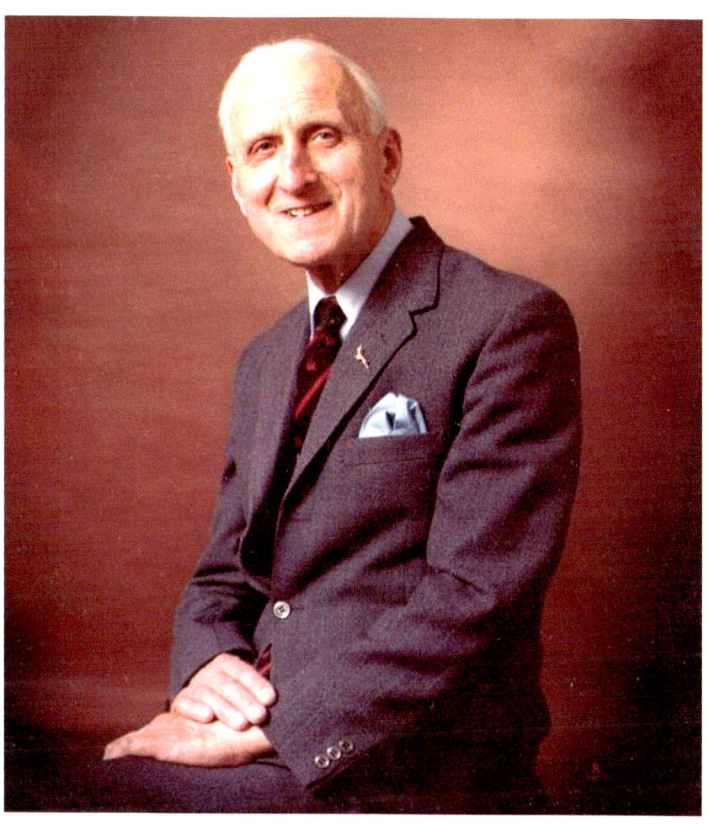

Gwynne Morgan. (WJ)

produced a number of Welsh internationals. Carmarthen Athletic, formed in 1944, has also nurtured numerous famous Welsh international players including Roy Bergiers, who scored the only try in one of the greatest upsets in world rugby when Llanelli beat the New Zealand All Blacks 9-3 in 1972. Carmarthen Athletic's clubhouse collection is quite exceptional and features sporting memorabilia from many elite sporting personalities collected over six decades. As well as a remarkable collection of rugby union jerseys, it has shirts from other sports and 143 pairs of sporting shoes that the Guinness Book of Records has recognised as being one of the best in the world.

The collection has expanded beyond legends of rugby to include the footwear of other sporting stars. Among the collection are Gary Player, Lee Trevino and Jack Nicklaus's golfing shoes. You can also see Muhammad Ali and Henry Cooper's boxing boots, Bjorn

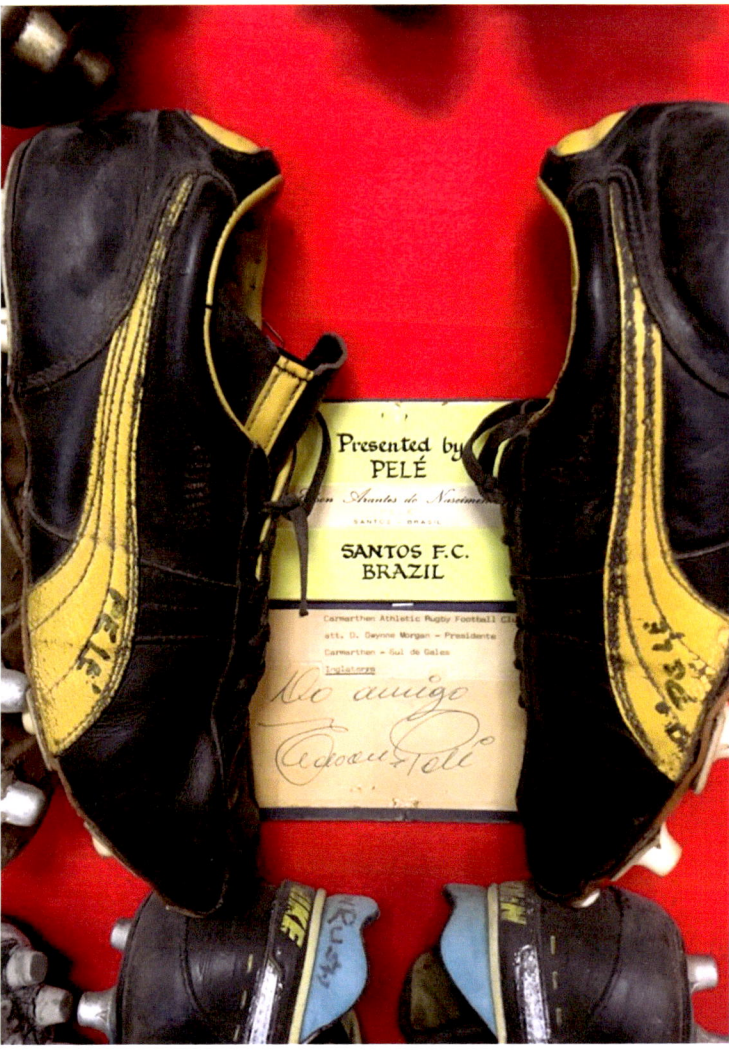

Pele's football boots. (WJ)

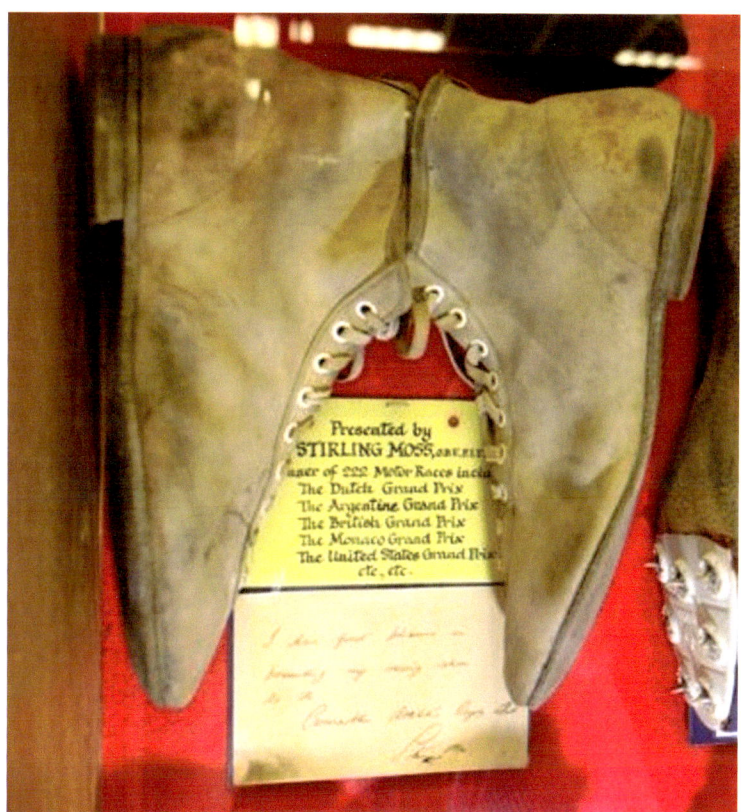

Stirling Moss's
diving boots. (WJ)

Borg, Billie Jean King and Ilie Nastase's tennis shoes, and Ian Botham, Viv Richards, and Gary Sober's cricket shoes. The football boots of Stanley Mathews, Pele and Franz Beckenbauer are also on view at the Athletic's clubhouse.

Started over fifty years ago by the club's then president Gwynne Morgan, who, with his brother Jack, ran King Morgan's chemist shop (established 1890) in King Street. The brothers mixed cough medicines following an age-old family recipe, which included chloroform, guaranteed to ease the most stubborn coughs and ensure a good night's sleep! The brothers were generous benefactors to local events and charities until their deaths in the 1990s, and the footbridge over the River Tywi near Carmarthen railway station is named Pont King Morgan in tribute to them.

The oldest outdoor concrete velodrome in continuous use anywhere in the world can be seen in the town park. During the 1890s cycling became an activity that provided newfound freedom for people, and by the turn of the century it had become a popular sport. The Carmarthen Park's Cycle Track, today known as the Velodrome, was modelled on tracks at Villa Park, Birmingham, and Crystal Palace, London, and measures 405.38 metres. It opened on Easter Monday in 1900 and was said to rival any in the UK. By 1901 accidents and bicycle thefts were commonplace and regularly featured in the

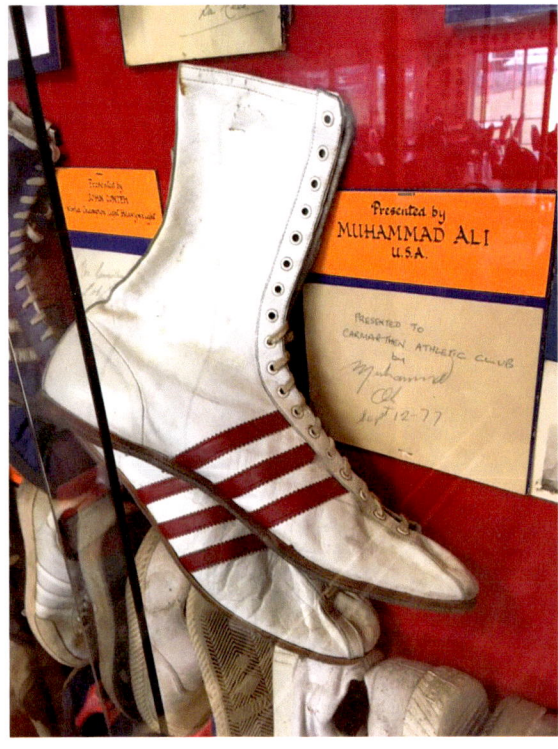

Mohamed Ali's boxing boots. (WJ)

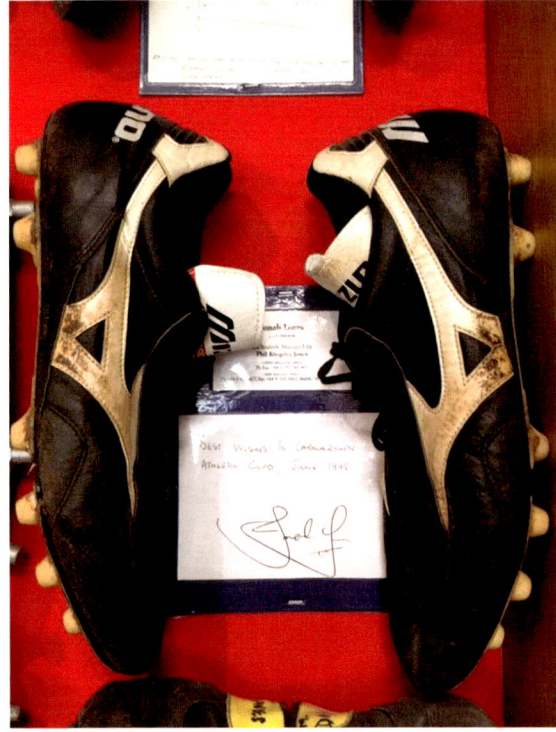

Jonah Lomu's rugby boots. (WJ)

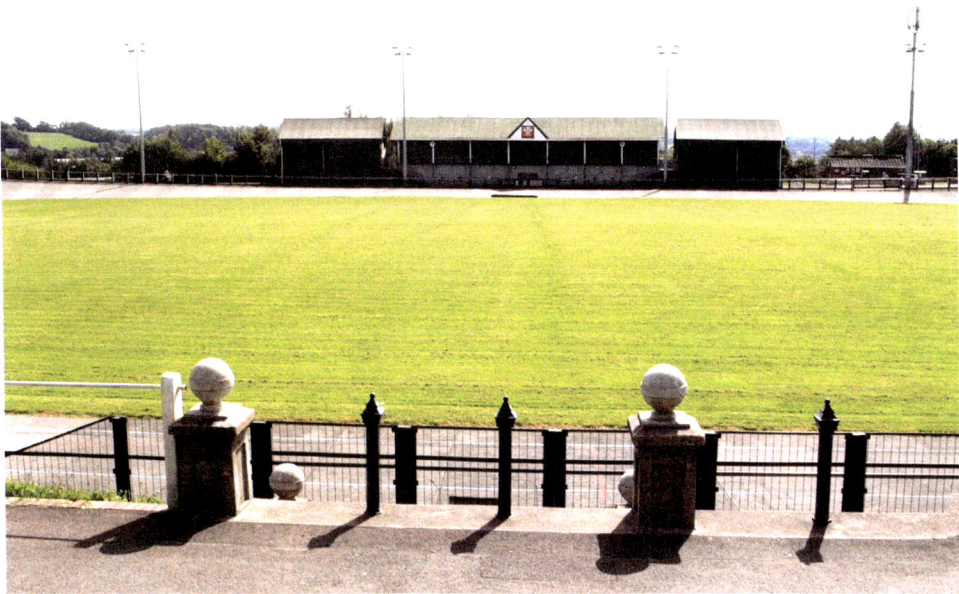

Velodrome.

local news, showing how popular the sport had become. It was there that the concept of 'pacing' was first introduced, where a cyclist achieved higher speeds by racing in the slipstream of a motorcyclist. After a £600,000 revamp, the velodrome was reopened in 2017 – just a year before Geraint Thomas, whose father hails from Bancyfelin, a stone's throw from Carmarthen, became the first Welsh cyclist to win the Tour de France.

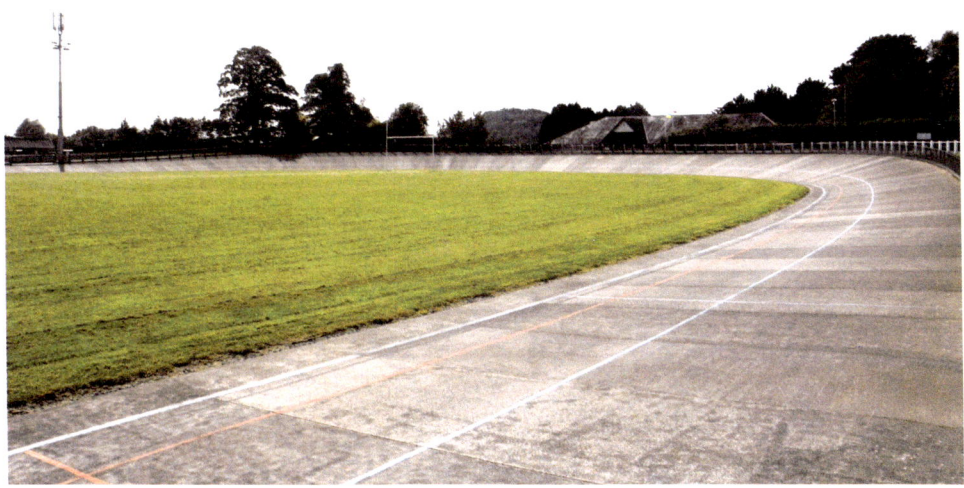

Velodrome.

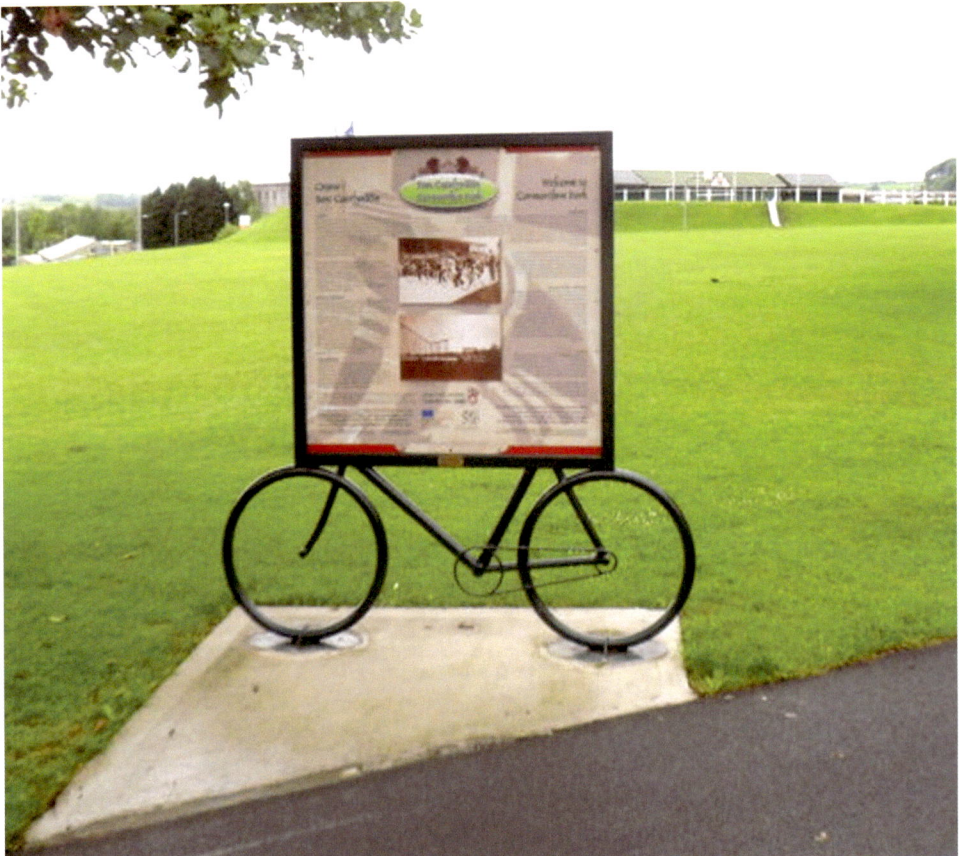

Velodrome information board.

Acknowledgements

In finding the primary sources needed to research and produce this publication I am thankful and indebted to the many wonderful and like-minded people who I have met along the way. Their help, guidance, generosity, and support as always has proved invaluable.

I am thankful to the staff of the Carmarthen Town Council, Eleri James, the Mayor Councillor Emlyn Schiavone, Councillor Wyn Thomas, Councillor Alun Leeny. Wynne Jones, Carmarthen Athletic Rugby Football Club, Carmarthen Library Services, Carmarthenshire Archives, Carmarthenshire Museum, and members of the Rushmoor Writers Group, without whom it would not have been possible to complete this project.

For allowing the use of their images I am obliged to Wynne Jones (WJ), Commercial Manager, Carmarthen Athletic RFC; Andrew Sellick, Commercial Operations Manager (Adran Cymunedau); Morrigan Mason, Carmarthenshire Museums and Arts Development Manager; Bassano Ltd; Geoff Charles, Friedrich Justin Bertuch (FJB), Graham Hogg, Henry Matthew Brock (HMB), Henry Gastineau (HG); Graham Hogg, Harry Payne and GeraintTudur2, CC BY-SA 3.0 Wikimedia Commons; Howard Pyle (HP); Jean Pierre Victor Dartiguenave (JPVD); John Duckfield; John Phillips; Lance Woodworth (LW); John Phillips, National Army Museum (NAM), Rose and Trev Clough; Richard Croft; Richard Caton Woodville Jr (RCW); (TJHSC) The John Howard Society of Canada; Richard Croft; and Van Henry Thomas Alken.

All other images are from the author's collection, in the public domain or free from copyright.

As always, I offer a special thanks for their continued meritorious support of me to my wife Maria, for keeping me focussed and for allowing me to do what I love doing, and to my good friends 'Stormin' Norm Goodman, Mike Selcon, Aled Eynon, and S. Thomson-Hillis, all of whom have played an important role in my finishing this publication.

I am also thankful to Amberley Publishing for their continued support and for allowing me to bring history to life.

About the Author

Dean has had a lifelong interest in history and military history specifically. Following his father, grandfather, and great-grandfather he joined the army at sixteen, serving with the Royal Army Ordnance Corps for eight years as a supply specialist and physical training instructor in the UK, West Germany, and Falkland Islands, reaching the rank of corporal. Following this, he joined Surrey Police, retiring as a detective chief inspector. During the last twenty years, Dean has acted as a battlefield and historic sites guide in the UK and Europe, and is a member of the Battlefield Trust, Guild of Battlefield Guides, and the Western Front Association.

When he moved to Carmarthenshire in 2021, Dean was keen to learn about the military and social histories of the county, and the culture of west Wales. The learning curve has been steep and while climbing it he has written *Carmarthenshire's Military Heritage*. This is his seventh book in the Military Heritage series, preceded by Hampshire, Kent, Sussex, Farnborough, Berkshire, and Dorset. He has also written two other books for Amberley Publishing: *Secret Maidstone*, about his hometown in Kent, and *Portsmouth's Murders and Misdemeanours*.

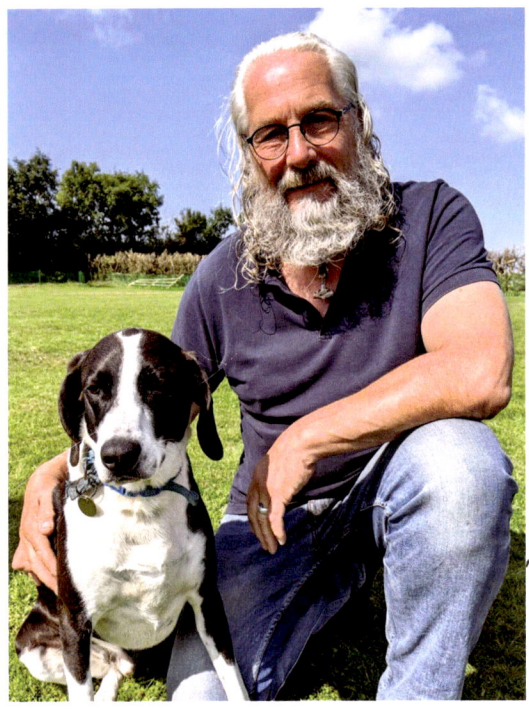

Dean with Gaius.